THE
ESCAPE
ARTISTS

THE
ESCAPE
ARTISTS

True Stories of People
Who Turned Their Obsessions
into Professions

JOSHUA PIVEN

McGraw-Hill

New York   Chicago   San Francisco   Lisbon   London   Madrid   Mexico City
Milan   New Delhi   San Juan   Seoul   Singapore   Sydney   Toronto

The McGraw·Hill Companies

1 2 3 4 5 6 7 8 9 0   DOC/DOC   0 9 8 7

ISBN-13: 978-0-07-147926-4
ISBN-10:   0-07-147926-0

McGraw-Hill books are available at special quantity discounts to use as premiums and sales promotions, or for use in corporate training programs. For more information, please write to the Director of Special Sales, Professional Publishing, McGraw-Hill, Two Penn Plaza, New York, NY 10121-2298. Or contact your local bookstore.

Designed by Nick Panos.

Photo credits: p. xviii © Jackie Taylor; p. 82 © Irene Donnell; p. 102 © Greg DeSanto; p. 146 © Tony Demin; p. 164 © Shelby Labario; p. 184 © Roy Toft; p. 208 © Kim Newby; p. 254 © Christine Piven.

What work I have done I have done because it has been play. If it had been work I shouldn't have done it.

—MARK TWAIN

CONTENTS

INTRODUCTION

I had no intention of jumping out of the airplane. And I *certainly* did not plan on trying to land in the Los Angeles Aquifer.

At first—that is, before I actually saw the rickety little sky-diving plane and my frighteningly small proposed landing spot—it all seemed like a great big adventure. I had flown out to LA, stayed overnight, and then awoken at dawn for the two-hour drive to San Bernardino. Behind the wheel of the rental car was a producer for the TV newsmagazine *20/20*, a show that had invited me on to discuss the surprising success of my humorous survival manifesto *The Worst-Case Scenario Survival Handbook*. They would fly me out to the West Coast (*Wow, a free trip out west! Cool!*), put me up in a hotel (*Free hotel room! So what if it's cheap!*), and I would get to talk about my book on national television. (Need I say more? *Yes, I'll do it.*)

The producer had particularly enjoyed the chapter in my book on how to survive a jump from an airplane if your parachute fails to open. Would I be willing, he wondered, to demonstrate it for television?

At this point, it's probably important to note that this was back in 1999, before the reality television craze was responsible for getting anyone to do just about anything on TV for cash—or the hazy promise of (at least fleeting) stardom and the possibility of a job working for "The Donald." Though I wanted to be on television, badly, I did have some reservations about the safety of this stunt.

I had exhaustively explained to the producer that my books were actually based on research, on discussions with experts, who told me how to perform these dangerous activities. Joe Jennings, the guy we were going to meet, was a skydiving photographer and choreographer, a well-known stuntman who had directed and filmed dozens of TV commercials: geese drinking Pepsi, guys leaping out of planes chugging Mountain Dew and then landing on mountains and skiing down on snowboards. He was my expert, the guy who had given me the detailed survival information. I was just the, *ahem*, writer.

Staying Grounded

Driving toward San Bernardino, passing mile after mile of irrigated desert landscape on our way to the remote local airstrip, I began hedging. "I haven't actually jumped out of a plane with a faulty parachute," I noted helpfully. "Actually, I've never jumped out of a plane at all," I admitted. Hedging suddenly became furious backpedaling. "It's all really just a theory," I explained. "Not that I don't think it will work. I mean, I stand by all the information in the book." I wasn't sure if I was trying to convince the producer or myself. Or maybe both of us.

Then I played my trump card: "It's just that, well, you know. I'm only an *author*."

This was the first of what would turn into many moments of what I later termed "extreme self-awareness," when I admitted to myself that, though I occasionally played one on TV, I really wasn't a macho, adventurous, cigar-chomping, three-day-growth-of-beard, Tom Selleck–lookalike kind of guy. (OK, I did have a spotty three-day beard, but that was just because I was too lazy to shave.) That dude who got injured mountain climbing and had to cut off his own arm to survive? Well, that wasn't me. The blind guy who summitted Mount Everest? Clearly insane. Yes, I enjoyed the outdoors: riding my bike, the occasional ski vacation, a short hike with plenty of water, sandwiches, GPS equipment, and signal flares. In fact, I *did* know how to survive these crazy situations, but it was only in a bookish way. I was an adventurer, but of the armchair variety.

What it finally came down to was that I wasn't one of those people who did extraordinary, escapist things. I mean, yes, I had written a best-selling book about survival, which was very cool and tremendously exciting. But in describing myself for the about-the-author section, I had struggled to come up with something suitably thrilling and debonair. I eventually chose to describe a vacation to Jamaica during which I had been robbed at knifepoint. Pretty exciting stuff.

As we waited at the airfield for Joe Jennings to show up, I imagined what he might look like, having only interviewed him on the phone and via e-mail. I pictured him racing down the dirt track leading to our tiny airfield—perhaps driving a Chevy

Camino, one of those half-car–half-pick-up things from the seventies—dust clouds enveloping us as he slammed on the brakes and stepped out of his ride, one creased and cracked cowboy boot hitting the dirt and stomping out his filterless Lucky. At a tanned six-feet-four, he would tower over us as he slapped my back, practically knocking me over as he forcefully announced that it was "a great day for a jump."

As it turned out, Joe drove a Honda Accord. He was of average height, rather slim, and would soon be bald. And he didn't smoke. But he was enthusiastic as he described the stunt. He would jump first, a video camera mounted on his helmet. Then his two colleagues would jump. One would pretend he was having a 'chute malfunction, waving his arms and signaling to the third guy. The two would then link up while free-falling, the third guy would pull his ripcord, and the two would float down together, landing in the 40-foot-wide Los Angeles Aquifer. Joe would film the entire thing.

Was I ready to jump too, he wanted to know? Because I had no experience skydiving, I would jump "tandem," meaning I would be harnessed to another one of his guys, with nothing to do but enjoy the view and try to hold down my breakfast. "C'mon dude, it's a killer rush," he said. Yeah, I thought, "killer" seemed an apt description. Safe in my authorial cocoon, my mind drifting to my new bride—I had been married just a few months before—I demurred. Too risky, I quickly calculated.

As a compromise, I agreed to sit in the open doorway of the small plane as it roared down the airstrip, announcing to the camera and audience what was about to take place. The producer would yell "Cut!" and I would hop out before the plane took off. Except that I kept forgetting my lines. After five loud, dusty takes, I got everything right, the plane stopped, I got off, Joe and his crew got on, and they took off.

The stunt, I was told later, went off without a hitch. I missed it because I had to leave early to drive back to LA and catch my flight home. The closest I got to actually jumping out of a plane was watching it from my couch a few weeks later; they had sent me the videotape.

Extraordinary People

Looks can be deceiving. Joe Jennings was clearly an extraordinary guy, taking major risks while doing something he loved to do. And he was successful, which obviously made it even more rewarding. I got to thinking about people like Joe not too long ago, in the course of writing another book, which was on space travel. I was following the launch of *Space-ShipOne*, the new "commercial" spacecraft built by legendary aircraft designer Burt Rutan and financed by Microsoft jillionaire Paul Allen.

SpaceShipOne was the most successful craft in what its creators hope will be a new wave of private space travel tourism. Using an entirely new (and untested) form of rocket propulsion, the ship would leave Earth's atmosphere and travel in space for a few minutes, offering those on board a short period of weightlessness before returning to Earth. After two successful test flights, *SpaceShipOne* was awarded the Ansari X PRIZE, a $10 million grant set to be given to the first privately developed and financed spaceship that reached orbit on two separate occasions. Upon its return, Sir Richard Branson, of Virgin Atlantic Airways fame, announced his company would license the *SpaceShipOne* design and begin building spacecraft for the company's new venture, the cinematically named "Virgin Galactic." The expected price for a two-hour journey to space on a Virgin Galactic flight: $110,000.

While the idea of a private spaceship flinging movie stars and the rest of the superrich into orbit seemed cool, I guess, I was less interested in the craft itself than in Brian Binnie. Binnie was the guy who actually agreed to pilot *SpaceShipOne*, perhaps the most experimental and dangerous private aircraft ever built. Not only did the ship use a new type of rocket engine and propulsion system (it literally burned rubber), but it would break the altitude record set in 1963, actually entering low Earth orbit, floating for a while, and then sinking back to Earth in the same manner as a badminton shuttlecock.

Why in the world would someone agree to take the controls?

Sitting in a hard-backed Starbucks chair one frigid morning a few weeks later, struggling with my space book manuscript, it occurred to me that Brian Binnie and Joe Jennings, while doing different things, were a lot alike. They were people with extraordinary pursuits that they loved. As a writer, I too was doing something that I really loved. But my job had me slumped over a computer drinking overpriced lattes. These guys were doing incredibly cool, fun, often-dangerous things. I wondered, were they getting rich? Did they even care about money? What did their wives and kids think of their jobs? Did they worry about dying? Had they left boring jobs to do these things? How long had they known what they wanted to do? And what drove them to pursue it?

Then I thought about all the hundreds of people I had interviewed over the past eight years: the CIA agents, coroners, surfers, wild animal trainers. The firefighters, scientists, and extreme skiers, the trauma surgeons, bodyguards, stuntmen. They too were passionate about what they were doing, even (or maybe especially) if it was something really unusual or dangerous.

The Great Escape

I began to wonder what drove these people and what, if anything, they had in common. I of course knew what they did. But I didn't know *why* they did it. In essence, I wondered what made them tick. In my mind, I began referring to them as my "escape artists." The term popped into my head because they reminded me of Walter Mitty, the protagonist of James Thurber's famous short story "The Secret Life of Walter Mitty." Walter Mitty was a character stuck in a humdrum life who constantly daydreamed of escaping to something better, something more exciting, something extraordinary. As the author of survival handbooks, I had always imagined myself in dangerous or daring situations, even though—as my skydiving episode painfully revealed—I was basically content to be an armchair adventurer with an occasional trip to Great Adventure. But here were all these real-life escape artists, people doing cool, crazy, dangerous, sometimes seemingly adolescent or purposeless tasks, and having a great time doing them. They were people following their dreams, pursuing their passions, often at the expense of material gain.

I surmised that there had to be thousands—perhaps hundreds of thousands—of people out there for whom working in an office or a cubicle was a fate worse than death (I was one of them). Young people graduating from high school or college, slightly older people looking to do something more creative and fulfilling with their lives, people who wanted an escape from the everyday. What might I learn about my own life, about my potential future, from talking to them about why they did what they did? And what might someone else learn? Admittedly, I wasn't sure. What could one learn from a circus clown? Or a Trekkie? Or a surfer? Were they happy, or merely content? I hoped to find some answers to these questions, and in my mind the book you're holding began to take shape.

What I wanted to discover were the reasons (personal and professional) people were rejecting the "workaday" nine-to-five life. In essence, I wanted to know about the extraordinary: unusual people doing really cool things, really *different* things. What was it like to be a baseball pitcher or a stand-up comic or a DEA agent? What was the life like? I hoped to draw some connections and conclusions—assuming there were some to be made—about what these people had in common, or didn't. I definitely had some ideas (my job, after all, was fairly nontraditional), but I hoped my own experiences would shape, not color, my argument.

To be honest, for me, much of the fun was in the doing. Tracking these escape artists down, talking to them, and learning about their lives seemed like a good way to spend my time. In doing so, I hoped to write an interesting book about people who do really interesting things, and why they do them. And I hoped to show that working at something you're passionate about can make "work" a whole lot more fun.

You'll decide if I've succeeded.

JOSH PIVEN
September 2006

1

FROM FANDOM TO
THE FINAL FRONTIER

ESCAPE ARTIST: RICHARD COYLE
GREAT ESCAPE: WHERE NO ONE HAS GONE BEFORE

Stardate 2285, on the Surface of the Planet Ceti Alpha VI

Initially, the planet had seemed perfect.

Upon their arrival, Commander Chekov and Captain Terrell thought the sixth planet of the Ceti Alpha star system was uninhabited—a forlorn, lifeless rock that might hold some interesting mineral samples but little else.

For once, this was a good thing. The planet seemed an ideal candidate for Project Genesis.

The two officers had beamed down to the planet's barren surface from the *U.S.S. Reliant*, a Federation starship involved in the top-secret Genesis project. Genesis would be a technologically advanced, revolutionary attempt to bring failed planets back to life, to make green what was once little more than sand and rock baked solid by nearby stars. But Genesis, Chekov knew, carried its biblical name for a very good reason. In creating life, it would first destroy every living thing on the planet—that is, if anything were alive down here to begin with. That's why it was critically important—indeed, essential—to take a complete survey of the planet, to make absolutely certain that there were no life forms hidden beyond the reach of the *Reliant*'s scanners. So the two men had beamed down to scan it from the ground.

But, Chekov now wondered, if the scanners were correct and the planet was barren—if Ceti Alpha was a "dead" system and a potential target for Genesis—why were they now standing in front of a series of well-worn cargo containers? And how was it possible, Chekov wondered fleetingly, that one of the containers contained a group of refugees from the Eugenics Wars of 1990s Earth? Even more perplexing was how the group's vicious leader, a notorious rebel and murderer, had managed to survive. It was all too incredible, too impossible. Yet it *was* possible because it was happening.

But no matter. Now it was far too late. They were trapped. There was no time to get on his wrist communicator (his "comm") to send a warning to the *Reliant* or to the Genesis scientists on Space Lab Regula One. No time to tell the ship to forget about him or about Captain Terrell. No time to instruct the crew to immediately and totally destroy the planet from orbit.

Chekov didn't bother to reach for his phaser. He had no illusions about blasting his way out, no dreams of possible escape. And he had no expectations of receiving mercy. Thoughts like these didn't occur to him. In fact, as he faced what he had absolutely no doubt was his end, one word, and only one word, went through his mind:

Khan.

Give the Man His Props

Sitting in the darkened theater, Richard Coyle knew without a doubt that Chekov, of course, would survive. Perhaps a little worse for wear, but he would make it.

Captain Terrell, on the other hand, was a goner.

Not immediately, Rich knew, but eventually: The actor who portrayed Terrell (Paul Winfield) was just too well known to die so early in the film. Terrell was no Yeoman Johnson, *Star Trek*'s proverbial sacrificial lamb, the show's stock character in virtually every episode whose sole purpose was to accompany a regular cast member to a new planet and be killed off in the first five minutes.

Rich watched with rapt attention as Terrell was infested with parasitic "Ceti eels," which would burrow sickeningly into his ear canal and through which the villainous Khan—portrayed by the inimitable Ricardo Montalban, at the height of his *Fantasy Island* fame—would control Terrell's mind, ordering him to kill Admiral Kirk. And he knew that Terrell, in resisting Khan's mind control, would ultimately turn his phaser on himself rather than kill Kirk. It was an effective plot development, Rich felt—suitably scary; futuristic, yet believable. And the Ceti eels, which looked like well-armored leeches, or perhaps miniature armadillos, were interesting.

Easing further back in his seat, enjoying the coolness of the theater, Rich wasn't the slightest bit worried about Chekov—or poor Captain Terrell, for that matter. He was more concerned with the look of those wrist comms. He was hoping they would get an all-important close-up, a shot that would show all those working LEDs and displays crammed inside those tiny cases. He hoped for a shot that would give the comms their big scene and would perhaps help them become part of "Trek legend."

But it didn't happen. He didn't get the shot; at least, not then. He had spent days designing and building the wrist comms in his workshop, by hand, along with many of the other props used in the film. He truly felt his props were ready for their close-ups. And not because he wanted the recognition, necessarily.

But because he was a *huge* fan.

The Obsessed

There are, of course, millions of *Star Trek* fans. There are probably tens or perhaps even hundreds of thousands of hard-core aficionados in what is known in Trek circles as "fandom." Most of these "Trekkies"—or "Trekkers" as many prefer to be called—grew up watching the original show in reruns, became equally obsessed with the *Star Trek* movies (of which, according to a widely held Trekkie belief, only the even-numbered ones are any good), and went on to obsess over numerous sequels and tangentially related TV shows such as *Star Trek: The Next Generation*, *Deep Space Nine*, and *Babylon 5*.

But Richard Coyle didn't begin his career as a studio prop maker who simply ended up falling in love with *Star Trek*. It was actually the other way around. His life has followed a more circuitous and unlikely path, one that began when he was a young science fiction "freak" in 1950s North Las Vegas, Nevada. His science bent sent him into the dead-end TV repair business as an adult, wound its way through the *Star Wars* franchise, led him to his first *Star Trek* conventions, his first home-made costumes and model ray guns, and then finally handed him his ultimate escape: A phone call from a stranger, asking him if he might be interested in building props for the movies, and mainly for science fiction movies.

There's no magic formula for turning a hobby into a career, of course. Often it's simply a lucky break or a chance encounter that sets the wheels in motion. But even offbeat hobbies can morph into unusual careers with some shoe leather and hard work. Still, unchecked obsessions can play havoc with personal relationships even *before* they turn into jobs: Rich's obsession had unintended consequences for his marriage. But that's getting ahead of things. To really appreciate his journey to the "Final Frontier," you need to start at the beginning, with a geeky, asthmatic kid who was obsessed with Flash Gordon.

From Vacuum Tubes to Vulcans

Unlike most of today's Trekkies, Richard Coyle is old enough to have grown up watching *Star Trek* during its original network television run, from 1966 through 1969. He was born in 1948 in New Hampshire, to the somewhat unlikely pairing of a mother who was an English teacher and a father who was a trucker. The odd match made for a somewhat unusual child. Instilled by his mother with a love of reading, especially science fiction, Rich as a youngster had a fairly advanced command of language (the mixed blessing of living with a high school English teacher), and he found that if he wasn't careful, he could easily "talk above" his peers. His father's wanderlust resulted in a family dragged across the country, often pulled by a 1952 Chevy pickup towing a 35-foot mobile home thousands of miles. The family moved around a lot, staying for a few years at then-remote places like Reno and Las Vegas. With little money, the Coyles usually ended up living in dusty, forlorn trailer parks on the outskirts of towns. Young Richard often found himself at odds with the children living around him, a little too smart in many ways and never in one spot long enough to fight things out or make lasting friendships, always the odd new kid in the park.

The desert states of Nevada, New Mexico, Arizona, and Colorado were a hotbed of UFO sightings and alien abduction tales in the late 1950s, and there was a general sense that people who took much interest in outer space were eccentric weirdos, if not full-fledged wackos. "In the 1950s," Rich recalled, "science fiction was definitely *not* cool." Afflicted (though at the time not diagnosed) with severe allergies and recurring, debilitating asthma attacks, afraid to talk about his science fiction passion with other kids, Rich instead lost himself watching early sci-fi TV shows like *Rocky Jones Space Ranger*, *Flash Gordon*, *Twilight Zone*, and *Outer Limits*. He spent countless hours on his tiny bunk bed in a cramped trailer poring through the novels of Robert Heinlein. "*Have Spacesuit, Will Travel* was probably my all-time favorite book," he remembered. "It was all about this kid who wins a secondhand spacesuit in a contest and goes all over the universe with it, and of course saves the earth and humanity!" Heinlein, often referred to as the "father of science fiction," wrote many of the books that later came to define the genre, including the groundbreaking *Stranger in a Strange Land* and *Starship Troopers*. (Oddly, he also invented the water bed.) "Heinlein was a huge influence on me because he wrote 'juveniles,' these wonderful sci-fi stories that usually had kids or teens as the protagonists, which were a great read for a teen," Rich said.

Unfortunately, like many young men of the era, Rich's life was interrupted by the war in Vietnam. "I was 19 in 1967, and not being in college, I was 1-A, virtually assured of getting drafted," he said. At the time, the thinking held that it was better to enlist than be called up. "I did not want to fight in the war, knowing my health was poor, and that I did poorly in what little sports I had done in school, so I figured by enlisting I might be able to get a noncombat posting." As it happened, his frequent asthma attacks made it nearly impossible for him to make it through basic training, and he was repeatedly hospitalized with upper respiratory infections. (However, during his Christmas furlough, Rich married his high school girlfriend.) The Army, after two more tries, finally got him through basic and then sent him to Fort Gordon, Georgia, to learn to operate the Teletype. Arriving on the verge of another illness and hospitalization, he was unable to complete even this physically undemanding training. It soon became apparent that he was not cut out to be a soldier.

Returning home with a wife and now out of the service, Rich fell back on the job he had been doing out of high school, working as a gas station attendant. In the 1950s, with the automobile storming the country, such jobs were widely available, and he became "one of those guys who came out and filled your tank, washed your windows, and offered to check your oil in the hope of selling you some, or finding other service work you needed." He also performed minor automotive repairs, a skill he had picked up as a kid in a family with little money to spend on such extravagances.

He began jumping around from job to job at gas stations ("Changing jobs was the only way to get a raise, and the other stations loved stealing someone's worker," Rich said), now with son Robert and daughter Karen, and he thought about trying to buy a shop of his own. "I was looking for some kind of business that I could own, where I could work for myself," he recalled. "I was of the generation that learned to work early. At 10 I was doing yard work, mowing lawns; at 12 I got a paper route; at 14 I had worked up to a scooter route, with more than 100 customers." But with a wife and two kids, he soon found gas stations were not willing to pay a living wage (at one point he was earning $2 per hour), and he was forced to work 60-hour weeks just to make ends meet. He visited a local employment office looking for a way out and was informed that he qualified for a program called "Vocation Training," and he was sent to a trade school for training in heating and air-conditioning.

But in Phoenix, he soon found, such a career presented a problem. "The summers were great, with constant work installing and fixing air-conditioners," he remembered, "but the winters were dead. There was just no work putting in heating systems in the desert. The work was way too seasonal for me. I had work for only about five to six months out of the year." Though he picked up valuable mechanical and electronics skills that would later serve him well, he was tired of work that was feast or famine. So, once again, he changed course, and he went back to the employment office hoping for something better.

Already a huge fan of television, Rich saw opportunity in TV repair. "You have to remember, in the 1970s, people still had these wood cabinet TVs with vacuum tubes, and these things would burn out once a year," Rich said. With his electrical and mechanical training, it was relatively easy for him to learn electronics and TV repair, and since most manufacturers used universal tubes, the repair path was clear: He could buy tube stock in a kit for a thousand bucks, get a picture tube tester and a pickup truck, and go into the TV repair business. The choice seemed like a smart one. Particularly in the desert southwest, people would stay in their air-conditioned homes and watch hour after hour of TV during the sweltering daylight hours. It was a great gig, for a while. Color TVs were all the rage, and there was a booming business in selling and fixing used color televisions.

But the job had other, side benefits for a sci-fi fan: lots and lots of TV watching.

"I watched *everything*!" Rich laughed. "*Star Trek*, *Twilight Zone*, *Outer Limits*, *The Man from U.N.C.L.E.*, this show about a robot called *My Living Doll*—really anything I could, lots of reruns even then. I remember that I had put up this huge antenna on the roof of my house. *Star Trek* played locally in Phoenix, and then 30 minutes later, a Tucson station would show another episode in reruns. Almost immediately I discovered that if I ran out and repositioned the antenna just as the early show ended, I could grab the Tucson signal. I quickly added a powered antenna rotator to allow me to turn the antenna remotely inside the house. I would watch the local TV airing, and then a second rerun right after. Two hours of Trek a day!" Unfortunately, he almost immediately made a disappointing discovery. The Tucson station was cutting scenes to fit in more commercials.

He had already memorized the episodes.

Once Upon a Time . . .

In the late 1970s everything changed for Rich Coyle.

A confluence of two key events sent Rich down the path that would eventually cause him to leave his itinerant nine-to-five work life and make *Star Trek* his living. The first event was a change in the electronics industry.

As with gas stations in the 1970s, modern technology had finally caught up with television manufacturing. By the mid-1970s, manufacturers had progressed to solid-state electronics, eliminating the need for tubes that could be relatively easily (though not cheaply) replaced by technicians. "Starting in the 1970s, as a technician you had to buy all these special modules, which were specific to the manufacturer, and worse, these new solid-state TVs were not wearing out as fast as the old hot-tube-driven sets," Rich recalled.

"Service was dropping off yearly, and in some cases due to cheaper and cheaper color TVs, it was becoming cheaper for the consumer to just buy a new TV than to pay for a repair." The TV repair business, Rich realized, was on its last legs. He needed to find something else to do before the repair work dried up completely.

The second event occurred in 1977 and was, in one sense, much more prosaic. It was just a movie. But for millions of sci-fi fans like Richard, it was an event that would change their lives. It was to become a pop culture phenomenon. It was a watershed event in marketing and merchandising. It was a huge leap to technical and special-effects hyperspace. And, for fans of science fiction, it was much, much more. It was the instantaneous liftoff to legitimacy they had been craving for so many years. It was an almost casual shrugging off of the sci-fi stigma. And, perhaps most important, it offered a path to social acceptability.

It was *Star Wars*.

And it was *HUGE*.

There had been other successful science fiction films before *Star Wars*, of course, including the Kubrick classic *2001: A Space Odyssey*. But the impact of *Star Wars* can't really be overstated. It made hundreds of millions of dollars ($300 million by one accounting), and that kind of money demanded respect. It also offered the first real look at how special effects could be used onscreen to tremendous success. Its mythic overtones, its pitched battle sequences between good and evil, its memorable costumes and characters—even its stilted dialogue and mediocre acting—all played a role in the film's tremendous impact, both culturally and commercially. It also ushered in, for better or worse, the era of the movie tie-in, the now ubiquitous merchandising of Hollywood films. The toy company Kenner went on to make hundreds of millions on its *Star Wars* tie-ins, and George Lucas made billions. (It was a development that would both help and hinder Rich's career.)

The impact on science fiction fans, in particular, was different. The enormous popularity of the movie was almost like sci-fi's "coming-out party." With this one film, the public attitudes toward and the perception of sci-fi had been inextricably altered. All of a sudden it was OK to be a science fiction fan, to talk in public, in mixed company, about "blasters" and "light sabers," about "warp drives" and "'droids." It was actually *cool* to talk about space travel!

The success of *Star Wars* led Hollywood producers to begin throwing money at anything sci-fi. Some films, like 1979's *Alien*, became classics of the genre. Others, like *Star Trek: The Motion Picture*, released the same year, were less well received by critics. Part of the problem, no doubt, was that every new sci-fi film of that period—*The Ice Pirates*, *The Last Starfighter*, *Flash Gordon*—was, understandably, compared to *Star Wars*, and generally unfavorably.

But reports of warring cast members, a budget that had swelled to over $40 million, and a special-effects team that was fired halfway through production didn't help the new *Star Trek* film. Neither did the fact that there was no real villain to root against (a plot device that future sci-fi filmmakers realized was an essential piece of the genre).

Even Trekkies seemed disappointed. "Among fandom, there was another name for *Star Trek: The Motion Picture*," Rich said. "It was often referred to as 'Star Trek: The Slow Motion Picture.' I mean, it was just slow." And there was a very good reason the film, onscreen, seemed thrown together. It had been. Paramount had been working on reviving the *Star Trek* television show, intending on bringing back the original cast for a new TV run. With the outsized success of *Star Wars*, the studio decided to make a movie instead. Sets had already been built or partially built, and to save money—which was later overspent on special effects—the story line was shoehorned to fit a "big film."

But for Rich and other sci-fi fans, both *Star Trek: The Motion Picture* and *Star Wars* served as bonding mechanisms, a way for fans of the genre to celebrate its success.

"I remember the day I saw the *Star Wars* trailer. I could *tell*. I said 'I have to see this film!' It was unbelievable. It just didn't look like anything I had ever seen before. (And I *had* seen them all up to that point, even *Star Maidens*.) It looked so much better, so much more real." So he found himself in the first line to see the first showing of *Star Wars* at the Cine Capri in Phoenix. Then he saw it again. And again. And again. Twenty-five to thirty times in all. "Whenever I had to go into town to get TV parts, I would time my trips so I could catch another showing," Rich recalled. "I mean, this was way before VCRs. You couldn't watch movies in your home in 1977, so if you wanted to see a movie more than once, you went to the theater." *Star Wars* played at the Cine Capri, nonstop, for a year.

The thing that would forever change Richard's life happened at that very first showing of *Star Wars*. While leaving the theater after the *Star Wars* screening, Rich spotted a flyer posted on a wall. It advertised a *Star Trek* convention (a "con") that was coming to Phoenix. George Takei (Lt. Sulu on the show) would be there, as would a few other cast members. But for Rich, the name of one special guest jumped off the page. Robert Heinlein was scheduled to appear. Instantly, Rich knew he would attend.

Getting Outed

Star Trek cons had been around for some years by then, but they really enjoyed their heyday in the late 1970s through the 1980s. "I remember I walked into my first con, and I got to shake hands and talk with Robert Heinlein, which was really great, a highlight of my life. But then I looked around and I saw all these people in costume, people dressed like *Enterprise* crew members and Klingons, and characters from other sci-fi shows," Rich said. "You have to understand what this was like for me. I had been a social outcast, a techno-geek, in hiding most of my life. In the past, I had worn a tiny—and I mean tiny—*Star Trek* insignia on my shirt collar. When I would run into someone else wearing one, we'd have to go off in secret to talk about the show, so we wouldn't be ostracized. Or beat up by the school bullies. It was almost like we were criminals. But here were all these people, these fans, celebrating openly," he said. "It was like I had found heaven."

Immediately excited about the "costuming," Rich learned it took two distinct forms in fandom: hall costuming and masquerade costuming. Hall costumes were less elaborate, typically the tight bodysuits worn by *Enterprise* crew members. ("If anything led to my total downfall, hall costuming was it!") Masquerade costumes were typically those depicting the show's aliens or odd life forms, with full headpieces and prosthetics, and full space suits—full "Darth Vaders." These outfits were too big and hot to wear all day, so each con had a "ball" for judging the best masquerade costume.

Though he was no tailor, upon getting home Rich immediately set about making a costume for himself. Cutting and pasting from various items around the house, he put together a Flash Gordon outfit: A T-shirt with a lightning bolt, a shiny black gun belt three inches wide, and bloused black pants. Black "Beetle" boots completed the ensemble. But his pièce de résistance was a "working" ray gun. "I took a toy Johnny Eagle Mugumba automatic pistol made by Topper Toys; I pulled off the slide and replaced it with a rounded compact dynamic microphone body." He then dissected a Meco *Star Trek* communicator electronics board to get at the beeping sound part and then hooked it up to the inside of the microphone body with an aluminum knob from a 10-turn pot so that he could change the sound. "I added an aluminum radio knob drilled out, and stuck in a plastic rod and a light on the barrel," he said.

Finally, he attached the gun to his hip with the microphone's hanger. It was an invisible "mystery holster," and it looked almost exactly like the ones used on *Star Trek*. He called his creation the "Beldorn Blaster." (The name was an inside joke. Rich liked the geekish irony of calling a big, "powerful" ray gun a "BB gun" for short.)

At his next con, he decided to enter the masquerade contest. His Flash Gordon get-up garnered hoots and hollers—most of the audience was too young to remember the German-made TV show of the early 1950s that Rich had watched as a child. And, apparently, his costume's lack of a *Star Trek* or *Star Wars* theme didn't help his case. A touch peeved, Rich pulled his Beldorn Blaster from its holster and began "shooting" at audience members, especially the hecklers, and the jeers turned to wild applause. "Remember, this was back in 1977, and a 'working' ray gun was almost unheard of," Rich said. After the ball (he didn't win), conventioneers crowded around him. Where had he found that gun? He had made it *himself*? Could he build more? How quickly? How much would one cost? Fans and dealers wanted to buy (and in many cases resell) them.

Later, trying to walk through the dealer's room, Rich was repeatedly stopped and asked to show off the only working ray gun at the con. "The dealers there didn't know whether to love me or hate me," he remembered. "I was drawing these huge crowds everywhere I stopped, but I was also taking business away from them: A mob looking at a ray gun was not buying comic books."

Up to this point, Rich had never thought of himself as a prop maker or wondered about becoming one. He had always been good with his hands and electronically savvy, but it had never occurred to him that there might be people willing to pay money—a lot of money—for ray guns and replicas of the gear used in their favorite movies. Suddenly, it was as if a gate in front of a long-closed road had been magically opened. "I began to build the blasters as fast as I could, and then I traveled to cons, many in California, to sell them. I was getting $100 to $125 apiece, but I was only able to build five or six in time for a con at first. And it took weeks to make them."

A Mixed Marriage

The cons were something to see: a sci-fi stew of kids, adults, hobbyists, curiosity seekers, and serious dealers making serious cash. And the activity wasn't limited to the convention halls. "I remember there used to be 'blaster wars' after hours, with all these costumed fans running around 'shooting' each other," Rich laughed. The "battles" would even spread to the cheap hotels surrounding the convention centers, with fully kitted-out "heroes" and "aliens" chasing one another in dank, shabby motel hallways and parking garages. Things got so bad that in the middle of the night, the airline flight crews who stayed at these hotels would complain about the noise.

By 1979, Rich was sometimes hitting two conventions a month, often away from home for a week at a shot, making enough money to finance the next trip. While con-going was tremendous fun, Rich came to realize he was spending a lot of time on the road and a lot of money paying for space on dealer tables, hotel rooms, gas, and upkeep on his van. As much as he loved going to the cons, he also had a wife and children at home that he needed to support. Seeking a better path to steadier income with less travel, at one con he caught up with an editor at *StarLog* (a sci-fi fanzine) and made a pitch: Rich would wholesale the Beldorn Blasters to the magazine, which would in turn sell them in its pages. A well-placed ad led to a flood of orders.

But all the travel, especially around the holidays (always the best times for a con), and lack of real money began to take a toll on his marriage. The *StarLog* deal, though promising, had come too late. By 1980, his wife had made an ultimatum: Stop the "silliness" or they would separate.

"We had always been in what's known in fandom as a 'mixed marriage,'" Rich said. "I was a sci-fi fan, and Sharon definitely was not. She had tolerated my obsession early in the marriage, but when it began to really take over my life, that was the last straw. But by that time we had nothing in common but the bills and the kids anyway." Sharon's initial idea was for her and the kids to live in one section of their duplex and Rich to live in the other, the one in front with his workshop. But Rich, tiring of this arrangement, made a few calls and soon took off to stay with sci-fi friends in LA, the center of West Coast fandom. At that point, both Rich and Sharon realized the marriage was essentially over. "It was your standard divorce. She got the house and the kids; I got what I could fit in my van." Rich loaded up the rest of his tools and equipment and drove back to California, to be closer to the center of the con universe. He lived out of his van, or crashed on the sofa of another fan.

If You Build It, They Will Con

While his personal life was in turmoil, professionally things were about to take off. In early 1981, he received a phone call from a guy who had tracked him down through a dealer at a *Star Trek* con. The man worked for a company, based near Los Angeles, called Modern Props. Modern Props was an outfit that built and then sold (or rented) props to movie studios. Large studios typically built their own large sets, which could be dismantled and reused, but they often subcontracted out the more specialized prop work. Modern Props had found this niche, and it had made many of the specialty props used in sci-fi TV shows and movies.

The man wanted to know if Rich might be interested in building some new props for Modern Props' next job, the second *Star Trek* movie, called *The Wrath of Khan*. His tasks would include building communicators and the drivers for the consoles and wall units used on the bridge of the *Enterprise*. For Rich, it was the opportunity of a lifetime. Though he was scraping by on his income from the con circuit, he now had a chance to be an insider, to get on the sets, to read the scripts, to build the toys! "It was amazing," Rich said, "and what was great about it was that very often, it was actually easier to build the movie props" than his own Beldorn Blasters, since typically the sound effects he had added to his Blasters were all handled by the special-effects department, not the prop makers. What's more, while a Trekkie could be highly demanding and exacting about his gear, Rich found the studios less so: They could always change camera angles or alter lighting to make props look their best or hide any flaws. Rich built numerous props for *Star Trek II*, including Chekov's and Terrell's special wrist comms, "Bones" McCoy's medical probe, light sticks, various electronic drivers for the consoles in the Regula One Genesis lab, Kirk's "box" communicator, and many others.

Unfortunately, the work on Trek props didn't pay very well either, and Richard and his girlfriend Jackie (a fellow fan he had met in Los Angeles, now his second wife) lived out of Rich's 1974

Chevy van, which they parked in front of the woodworking shop. "We used the building's bathroom and took sponge baths out of the shop sink," Rich recalled. "I had a 19-inch Zenith color TV in the van, and a bed, so we were not too hard up, and after all I was doing Trek, so I was very happy at the time."

Rich discovered that what he assumed would be a side benefit of working in the movie business—visiting the sets—could also serve to dampen the "magic" of moviemaking. "It does kind of disturb your enjoyment of the film, the suspension of reality, once you've seen how crudely made most of these sets are," Rich laughed. "The *Star Trek* skit on *Saturday Night Live*—with the old clothes wringer feeding paper through the wall to look like an automatic printout—was just about dead on!"

The work on *Star Trek* led to prop jobs on many other movies and TV shows, including *Knight Rider* and the short-lived but cult favorite *The Greatest American Hero*. But the real joy came when he was asked to make props for the *Star Trek* franchise, which continued to snowball. Rich went on to build countless props for Trek movies, including *Star Trek IV* (he made the famous "Klingon hand disruptor"), *V*, and *VI*, and the television shows *The Next Generation* and *Deep Space Nine*.

Possession with Intent to Distribute

Inevitably, with the huge commercial success of the Trek franchise, things began to change in fandom. Viacom bought Paramount Pictures in 1994, and it immediately began cracking down on unlicensed Trek merchandise, issuing its infamous

C&Ds (cease-and-desist orders) by the box load. *Star Trek* products (uniforms, masks, "weapons") that were once whimsical mock-ups of the beloved originals were now fraudulent, pirated goods, endangering the sales of the original things (themselves mock-ups of props from the 1960s TV show). "The whole deal with the C&Ds, the copyright infringement lawsuits and the policing, it all just took the fun out of it," Rich said regretfully. The overenforcement began to take on almost comic undertones. "I mean, they were busting 12-year-old kids running around with plastic phasers!" All of the "illicit" activity, the unlicensed sale of Trek products, had been tolerated by Paramount when it bolstered fandom and helped support the shows and movies—and, Rich said, the original *Star Trek* in particular owed its return to network television during its second year to the fans, who in a coordinated letter-writing campaign saved the show when it was about to be canceled.

But all of this changed when Viacom got hold of the studio, and it saw the lucrative potential in licensed merchandise and the amount of money the company was "losing" to "bootleggers." (No doubt Viacom executives had seen the hundreds of millions of dollars *Star Wars* merchandise had reaped for George Lucas and wanted this level of ownership and control.) Admittedly, the sale of Trek merchandise was not just the pastime of hobbyists and show fanatics—there were plenty of nonfans in the business with the sole intention of making a buck. And with the rise of the Internet came the ability to easily and cheaply buy and sell huge quantities of memorabilia across the globe. But the net effect of Paramount's enforcement action was a precipitous decline in the popularity of conventions. Dealers moved to the Internet—either to dodge enforcement or to broaden their customer base, or both—or got out of the business altogether to avoid steep fines. Though there are still a few cons and other Trek events today, all of the *Star Trek*–related television shows have ceased production, at least for now.

But Rich has found a way to continue pursuing his dream and still make a living. He now works with Roddenberry.com, the Web site run by Eugene Rodenberry, Jr., son of the late *Star Trek* creator Gene. Rich continues to design and sell show models and replicas, though he is now contemplating retirement ("if I win the Lotto," he noted). But he's never lost his love for all things sci-fi. "I'd really enjoy a new Trek series, though the new *Battlestar Galactica* is pretty fantastic. But I still love *Babylon 5*; it was one of the deepest and strongest shows done." (It's now off the air, but it is available on DVDs.) "It worked on so many levels, with these multishow arcs and characters developing over multiple seasons," he said. "I guess you could say it's kind of like our *War and Peace*."

To the Future—And Beyond!

Owning his own model-making business, running his own Web site (racprops.com, a site about movie and TV props and the business of prop making), Rich is happy to have lived his escape, happy to work for himself doing what he loves to do. "You know, I'm not rich, but I always made a living," he said finally. "Most of the other guys in this business come and go. I've stuck it out for 25 years now. I have traveled across the country many times, been to so many places, walked onto TV and movie sets, and watched them make movie magic. It has been a great life." Working with Roddenberry.com, Rich said, "is akin to a 'voyage home' for me. As in the beginning, I'm making props for fans."

WALL STREET MEETS SPECIAL OPS

Our passions, and our careers, can be ignited by influential figures in our lives. But just as a single important person can propel us forward, others around us can show us a path we'd like to avoid at all costs. Mark Divine's story is a little bit of both. It's a story of a man who became disillusioned with the actions of the people around him on Wall Street and who made a conscious decision to pursue a more meaningful life. But it's also a story about the impact of compelling people—and the martial arts—on one man's unusual career path.

Sometimes we keep moving in the same direction because we're too lazy or too busy or too fearful to try doing something else. We also have a tendency to stick with things into which we've invested lots of time and money—after all, it's only natural that we'd want to reap the benefits of our investments. It takes courage, and a bit of damn-the-torpedoes chutzpah, to change horses in midstream. But, on occasion, courage is exactly what's needed. Courage and, in Mark's case, some damn fine swimming.

The Soup Sandwich

This was bad. Really, really bad.

Mark Divine knew the boarding of the ship from below the waterline had become a classic "soup sandwich." It was something you couldn't get your hands around, something ugly and messy. A fouled-up mission.

He also knew there was little to be done about it. His men were tired—exhausted, really—and he was too. The water was frigid, hypothermic. It was pitch-black. Mark knew better than most platoon commanders that in the dead of night, cold tired men made mistakes. If you were lucky, the mistake could be caught and corrected, and the mission could continue. If you were unlucky, somebody got hurt. Or died. It was that simple. Most times, Mark knew, the difference between living and dying was that piece of luck, good or bad. But the one thing a Navy SEAL had going for him, the thing that could make the difference between living and dying, was the training. If you panicked and forgot it, you died. If you stayed calm and remembered it, you had a chance to live.

But the mission was blown—that much was clear.

It has started out as a textbook operation. Dive and swim underwater to the moored ship, and approach its hull from below. That was the first part. The second part was a little trickier. The entire SEAL team had to derig; that is, they had to remove their dive gear while underwater. Because all the equipment was too heavy to carry when they climbed onto the target vessel, it would be anchored to the steel hull of the ship, below the waterline, with strong magnets. The magnets were big and heavy, the size of dinner plates; they were the kind that were once used to attach contact limpet mines to ships. The operation called for the SEALs to remove their gear, gather it together below the surface, attach it to the magnets, and then attach the magnets to the ship. Then it was time to "blow and go": Pull out their regulators, exhale, and surface. After a successful boarding, they would return for their gear and swim away. That was what the textbook said, anyway. As if it would be 1, 2, 3, and out. As if it would be easy, as long as you followed the instructions.

The reality, Mark knew, was that it was never easy. The reality was that nobody could see anything, they were trying to communicate in the dark with hand signals, and there was too much gear. And everyone was freezing and tired. So tired, in fact, that someone had dropped one of the magnets. Had the SEAL team been lucky, the magnet would simply have sunk and settled on the bottom of the ocean. But this time, they were unlucky. The magnet had gotten caught in another man's rigging and pulled him straight down with it, a virtual anchor heading toward the sea floor. Worse, that SEAL had already removed his gear, including his breathing apparatus. Bad timing. And bad luck. As Mark counted the heads of his men, now bobbing on the surface, then double-checked again, he realized with a sickening feeling in his stomach what had happened. A SEAL was missing.

In his former life, on Wall Street, sitting at a desk in a suit and tie, he had dreamed of a more purposeful life, of accomplishing something. Of being a leader. But this was no wood-paneled boardroom, and there was no supple leather chair that squeaked when you sat in it. When you led here, the risks were not tallied in tall columns of figures. Mistakes were not reckoned in numbers or percentages but in failed missions, lives lost, and families destroyed.

Or in huge magnets that dragged an unlucky man down in the dead of night to the bottom of the sea.

Like a Fish to Water

Mark Divine had never imagined he would end up on Wall Street, much less command a platoon of Navy SEALs. In fact, growing up he had trouble imagining that he'd ever leave Barneveld, New York. A tiny town (perhaps "farm hamlet" is more accurate) of just 300 people outside Syracuse, Barneveld had been the family seat for the Divine clan since the 1890s, when Mark's grandfather founded Divine Brothers in nearby Utica. Divine Brothers was a successful (if somewhat less than glamorous) family business, a light manufacturing company that had once made the first wheels for Henry Ford's Model T—wheels made from sturdy canvas cushions, not rubber.

Born in 1963, Mark had grown up watching his father run the family business and his mother raise Mark and his three siblings. Barneveld was a place so small and out of the way that the public high school had to aggregate students from numerous middle schools in the area just to fill the classes. "The most popular organizations at the school," Mark remembered, "were the Future Farmers of America and the 4-H Club." Of the 225 seniors who graduated with Mark in the late 1970s, 4 would go on to college. Though it remained unsaid, it was all but expected that Mark would join his older brother—and, eventually, his younger brother—in running Divine Brothers after high school.

Aside from running a manufacturing company in farm country, there was something else that set the Divines apart from the other rural families in Barneveld: their second home. For Mark, the family's summer house on the western shore of Lake Placid was a refuge and a place that would change the trajectory of his life. "That's really where I became a water bug," Mark recalled. "I was swimming probably before I could walk. We were basically in the water all summer long, and we also had a motorboat that we would use for waterskiing. I remember my brothers and I would concoct all these crazy devices, and one of them was this sled that we dragged behind the boat, and we would lay on this thing and 'porpoise' it so the lip would catch, and then we'd dive down underwater. So we'd have our masks on, holding our breath underwater, and we were using this thing as basically an underwater swimmer delivery vehicle," he laughed. "Really early frogmen antics!" Though this was long before he even thought of joining the military, in retrospect he noted that it almost seemed "preordained" that he'd take to the water as a career.

But not before he became an accountant.

Mark was one of the four in his high school senior class to go to college. An extremely fit, six-foot-one, 190-pound, blond and blue-eyed young man, he was highly sought after as a high school swimmer, and he was actively recruited by several top schools, including Williams College. Though he had been told by that school's swimming coach that he was "as good as in," he was ultimately wait-listed, so he chose Colgate University in Hamilton, New York, instead. He swam competitively at Colgate for two years, and then he was offered a spot with a group of economics students that was headed to London for a semester to study at the London School of Economics. "It was a tremendous opportunity, and I guess that's where I was bitten by the finance bug, and it also opened my eyes to the potential of different careers outside the family business," Mark said. "Thank God!" Upon his return, he began swimming less and took up rowing instead, but he put most of his energies into lining up a summer internship in New York City, eventually landing a job with Coldwell Banker Commercial, a major real estate investment firm. It was good work experience, and it was enough to let Mark know that he wanted to work in Manhattan when he finished school. After senior year, he got his first job offer from the top accounting firm of Coopers & Lybrand— at that time one of the "Big 8" firms.

Though accounting has never been especially sexy, in those days working for one of the large firms was a solid and lucrative career, one untainted by the stigma of scandals that would come later. Though he had not taken any accounting classes as an undergraduate, Mark had a pretty good head for numbers. But the real draw wasn't the job as much as the perks. And the big perk was free education. At that time, the big firms had just instituted programs designed to attract liberal arts college graduates with finance or economics backgrounds by paying for their graduate school educations, which would culminate in master's degrees in accounting and qualification for the CPA exam. The theory was that the programs would mint loyal, well-rounded employees who might make good partners some day. (In practice, many accepted their free degrees and then promptly left the firms.) And there was yet another carrot that was dangled. After finishing up the master's program, Mark could stay in school for one more year and get his MBA, which he did. Mark began attending classes at NYU's Stern School of Business full-time in the summer of 1985, then went on a part-time schedule in the fall, when he began work at Coopers.

There was a downside to the job, however. He soon found that he hated the work and the schooling. "It was miserable. I despised it," he said, laughing. "But I'm not a quitter, and I had started it, and I knew that this was a good company, and it got me to New York City. Plus I was going to get my MBA essentially paid for, from a top-10 business school, and assuming I passed the exam, I'd have my CPA. So, three years out of Colgate I'd have an MBA, and I'd be a CPA, and I'd have some really, really good foundational work experience," he said. "It just seemed like a hell of a package deal. If I could gut it out."

It was during this hectic period that Mark started doing martial arts in order to find some balance in his life. "What got me through those years was really my martial arts training, which I took up as soon as I got to New York," he recalled. He began to train with Kaicho (Grandmaster) Tadashi Nakamura at Seido Karate, on 23rd Street in Manhattan. (It's still there.) Nakamura had founded his Seido style of karate 30 years before, as a spinoff from the traditional form of the art, which had been moving away from its more spiritual essence. In particular, training with Nakamura—whom he described as a mentor and a father figure—began to change Mark's outlook about the direction his life was going and his purpose. The training was rigorous, and he mastered the hand-to-hand combat skills that would be so important in the military. Mark fought in tournaments, and he did well. But unlike other forms of the sport, Seido did not stress such combat training, because doing so highlighted only the more physical aspects of karate, and Nakamura was uncomfortable with such a focus.

It's not unusual to hear about people whose self-confidence and outlook in life have been changed by (and through) the study of martial arts. Practitioners, especially those who train seriously and achieve a high level of proficiency, talk about seeing people and things in a different way. But for Mark, the training changed the entire course of his life. As he trained for his *shodan* (black belt), Mark also began regular Zen meditation, which led to an increase in his self-confidence and self-awareness; that is, as he put it, Zen meditation gave him the ability to listen to his "inner voice." It was this voice that would eventually lead him to change the direction things were heading. And it's clear that studying under Nakamura in particular played a major role in this change of priorities. Nakamura had created Seido—which roughly translates to "sincere way" in Japanese—to develop complete individuals, people committed to improving themselves and their communities. The principles of love, respect, and obedience were the foundation of Seido karate, and Nakamura wanted his students to develop spiritually and morally, as well as physically.

To his dismay, Mark would soon learn that in many cases his career in finance was incompatible with the Seido principles. Things began to change in 1987, the year of Black Monday, which was the largest stock market crash in history.

The Crash

In 1987, Mark left Coopers & Lybrand and began working for the highly respected accounting firm of Arthur Andersen. (The firm would split into two companies two years later, Accenture and Arthur Andersen, and the Arthur Andersen half would go down in flames with Enron in 2001.) He was auditing both large public companies and small private ones, and he was drawing a sizeable salary of $50,000 ($100,000 in current dollars) with the potential to go much, much higher. But he had chosen a world where mid-six-figure paychecks were routine, and where seven- and even eight-figure bonuses were not unusual. It was the go-go eighties, the flashy decade, the years personified by Michael Douglas's character Gordon Gekko in the film *Wall Street*. It was a time when "Greed was good. Greed worked."

One negative aspect of his job as an outside auditor brought in to check the books, however, was that Mark found he was often persona non grata. His presence at many companies was tolerated, but for the most part he was ignored by the employees around him. For them, he was simply an obstacle to making money, a cost of doing business. Mark recalled this period as disheartening and difficult.

"Some of these guys, these traders, would walk by you and—forget about acknowledging your presence—act as if they didn't even see you. I was like a ghost," he said. Among his clients at the time was the then-high-flying junk bond firm Drexel Burnham Lambert, led by the notorious trader Michael Milken. A year later, Milken would be sentenced to 10 years in federal prison for securities fraud and conspiracy; Drexel would be destroyed and file for bankruptcy in 1990. "There was just this entire subculture of greed and envy, of everybody's self-worth somehow tied to their paychecks," Mark recalled. In short, it was not a great time to look for role models in finance. "I had always seen myself as a leader," Mark said, "and I looked around me and did not see any leaders."

Then came the stock market crash. On October 19, 1987, the Dow Jones Industrial Average fell 22.6 percent, wiping out $500 billion in shareholder value. The years 1986 and 1987 had been banner years for the market, and as a result many stock market professionals had been highly leveraged to take advantage of the market's huge run-up. Later that day and the next, several brokers were shot and killed by irate clients who had lost everything; others committed suicide.

"Most of my clients were in the financial services sector, and it really was like *Bonfire of the Vanities*—these guys were king of the universe," Mark recalled. "And then the market crashed, and the crash really impacted me, that people could just be so tied to money and that their self-worth was just so tied up in their net worth or their salary. It just wasn't healthy."

If the market crash demonstrated greed on the macrolevel, the last straw for Mark was on the microlevel. Arthur Andersen had been called in by the IRS to audit a small company that was a privately held, family business. "This was basically an easy target for the IRS because the head of the company was using it as his own personal checkbook, but this guy was just completely naïve. He may have been breaking the law, but he just figured it was his business, he owned it, and he'd just let the accountants figure it out," Mark said. The IRS, however, took a dimmer view and brought in Mark's company for an audit. "This was probably a 2- or 3-person job that should have taken three weeks," Mark recalled, "and it became a nine-month job for about 12 people, and it just bled this company dry." Here was a company, much like the one run by his father and brothers, that had been destroyed by a drive to squeeze out every dollar, regardless of the cost or the consequences.

A month later, the owner died. "During the audit, the owner of the company got seriously ill, with cancer, and he passed away, while I was acting as one of these 'drainers,'" Mark said. "And I was just disgusted by the whole thing. I had seen this greed with my clients, and now I was seeing it on a corporate level. The system bled revenue wherever it could, without any regard to any sense of balance."

He knew it was time to make a change.

But Can You Swim?

Mark credits, at least in part, his martial arts training with showing him how people with character operated, and he knew he wanted to be that kind of person. "I wanted to be a leader, and I wanted to do something unique with my life. I wanted to do something that was going to be physically and emotionally challenging, something to get me out of this ruthless rut I was in." At the time, his brother was working with a former Navy SEAL, and Mark vividly remembered meeting the man and being impressed by his confidence, his sense of presence, and what Mark described as his "steely gaze." "I started to read about the SEALs after meeting this guy. His name was Jeff Schaeffer, and you could just tell he had been places and done things that the average person could only dream about, or read about. And I was intrigued."

Mark briefly considered joining the Marines or the Air Force, but his swimming background made the Navy SEALs the obvious choice. SEALs are paid by the Navy, but organizationally they are part of the armed services' Special Operations Command (SOCOM), which includes the Army's Special Forces (the Green Berets), the Delta Force, the 75th Ranger Regiment, and the Air Force's Special Ops. One important distinction is that while other Special Ops units are considered "force multipliers," often working for long periods deep undercover with indigenous forces, SEALs are strike teams. This means that they are trained to operate in very small squads (typically four- to eight-man groups) and to get into and out of enemy territory undetected. Operationally, SEALs are tasked with performing extremely fast, direct action missions without leaving a trace, with a rule of thumb that they always have "one foot in the water," meaning they operate in or very near water at all times. As such, Navy SEALs must be extraordinarily fit, and among their ranks are Olympic swimmers and many triathletes (including Mark, who ran and swam triathlons every few months for many years). SEALs are also specially trained in using explosives and conducting underwater demolition.

Without telling his parents, Mark began talking to a Navy recruiter. With a master's degree under his belt and a desire for leadership training, he began to think about joining the Navy at the officer level, which would require him to go to Officer Candidate School, or OCS. Unfortunately, he learned that virtually all Navy SEAL officers come from the Naval Academy and Navy ROTC—entering this special service from the civilian world at the officer level was, if not unheard of, nearly impossible. "There were like six or eight guys a year who were accepted into SEAL OCS as civilians," Mark said. "Today, it's even harder, probably harder, statistically speaking, than becoming an astronaut. As a civilian, you're better off enlisting in the Navy and then moving up through OCS" and into the SEALs.

In early 1989, Mark submitted his papers to the Navy. He still had not told his parents what he planned to do, mostly because he could imagine their reaction. "We were a typical northeast family, and northeast families don't usually have their kids join the military," Mark said. "When he was younger, my dad had served as a paratrooper for two years, and he was proud of that service, but he was a bit of a hell-raiser, and I think it was more the 'join the military or go to jail' type of service," he laughed. "We didn't talk about it much. We were not a military family, by any means."

That was about to change. At the end of the summer, Mark was scheduled for an interview with an active-duty commander named Woody Woodruff. Mark walked into a small room furnished with a desk and two chairs and met the gaze of Woodruff, a tan, blue-eyed, physically imposing figure in a uniform festooned with ribbons. Woodruff said nothing when Mark entered the room. Attempting to break the uncomfortable silence with small talk, Mark introduced himself and asked a few meaningless questions. Woodruff said nothing; he just stared at Mark, sizing him up. After several tries at conversation, Mark stopped talking. Still, Woodruff said nothing. For five minutes, the two men stared at each other across the desk in silence. Finally, Woodruff spoke.

"Mr. Divine," he asked, "have you ever been out of control in your life?"

Mark thought for several seconds before replying.

"No, sir," he said.

The man looked at him for a second before responding.

"Well," he said and paused, "you will be."

With that, the interview was over.

Phoning Home

Two months later, Mark's papers came through. He had been accepted at Officer Candidate School and was ordered to report to OCS, and then to Basic Underwater Demolition/SEAL training (BUD/S) in Coronado, California. (His salary would be $500 a month.) "That interview was the longest five minutes of my life." In retrospect, Mark felt that Woodruff was alluding to his upcoming SEAL training, where he would be in situations in which he'd have absolutely no control over the outcome. Which is also, of course, exactly what being in battle is all about.

Mark called his parents, and his mother picked up the phone.

"Mom," he said, "I've got something to tell you. I just joined the Navy to be a SEAL."

There was no response.

"Mom?" Mark said. "Mom, are you there?"

In seconds his father got on the line.

"Mark, what did you say to your mother? She's bawling right now."

"I told her I joined the Navy to be a SEAL."

"What? Why, Mark? Why? Why did you do this?" his father asked.

"I told him I was not happy with my life," Mark recalled. "That this was a decision that was internally generated. That I wanted to do something for myself, not for some expectation of what society wanted from me." Eventually, his parents came around to the idea. (Though not before his mother, in search of moral support, talked to some friends who helpfully informed her that SEALs were "those baby killers.")

In October, just before he left New York, Mark finally passed the CPA exam. He also received his MBA in finance, and he got his black belt in Seido karate. Then he quit his job, packed his bags, and headed for the West Coast.

Adult Swims and Sugar Cookies

Officer Candidate School was primarily classroom work, most of which, according to Mark, was "useless" in terms of becoming a SEAL. The real training started with BUD/S. BUD/S is an intensive program designed not just to teach and condition but to weed weaker men out of the SEALs.

The first phase of BUD/S is physical training, which begins with a hose-down with freezing water at four o'clock in the morning, as well as general verbal harassment from the instructors. In addition to 1-, 2-, 3-, and 6-mile timed swims, the recruits run everywhere, typically on runs of up to 5 miles but sometimes as long as 14. Much of the training is performed on little or no sleep, including one period (known as "hell week") where the men train for 24 hours each day over five days and nights, sleeping just 2 hours total. Highlights of this enjoyable period include low crawling through mudflats, running with boats carried on heads, and a 15-mile paddled-boat "tour" around Coronado Island, after three nights without sleep. The students are kept wet, cold, and sandy for the duration of hell week. (A student who falls behind during physical training runs the risk of a special humiliation: being soaked and then covered with sand—including under his arms, in his hair, and down his crotch—and being tagged a "sugar cookie.")

Mark found that as the weeks went by, the run and swim times were shortened and the training thus became progressively harder, all with the intent of forcing the weaker men to quit. Trainees would gather on the beach at the SEAL compound in Coronado, in a square known as "the grinder"—the purpose of which was to grind down a man's character to nothing so that it could be rebuilt. (A prominent sign in the compound reads, "The only easy day was yesterday.") Exercises included flutter kicks, endless push-ups, pyramid dips and pull-ups, and lunges. Pool exercises included "cross-overs," for which men are to swim 50 meters underwater fully clothed, and "drown-proofing," when a man's arms are tied behind him, his legs are tied together, and he is ordered to float for 10 minutes and then "swim" for 100 meters in freezing water. The exercise is complete when he dives to the bottom and picks up his mask with his teeth.

This training was interspersed with lessons on patrolling, weapons, explosives, and open- and closed-circuit diving. For closed-circuit diving, a rebreather is used to eliminate the air bubbles that might signal a clandestine diver's position. The training is often dangerous, and purposely so. One good example is the feared "rock portage." For this skill, students must paddle small inflatable watercraft through the surf zone—where the waves themselves may be dangerously large—and beach their boats directly onto rocks. Men are typically thrown from boats or smashed between their boats and the rocks, or they are simply heaved onto the rocks by the ocean. Sometimes, the instructors will wait for a particularly bad storm to barrel into Southern California before beginning rock portage. There are many injuries.

If staying in the program was difficult, quitting BUD/S was equally imposing. Getting out was purposely designed as a very scripted, very public humiliation. A bell sat in the center of the grinder. If a man could not continue with his training, he rang the bell, signaling his intention to give up. If they quit, men who had come up through the ranks could return to their previous Navy units. Men in Mark's position, however—men who had come from the civilian world—were washed out, finished. Typically, after just the first few weeks of training, about 30 percent of any given SEAL class has already "rung out."

Much of the final phase of BUD/S training takes place at Camp Billy Machen on San Clemente Island, off the coast of Southern California. (Among SEALs, Camp Machen is known as the place where "no one can hear you scream.") This phase teaches land navigation, rappelling, small-unit tactics, and marksmanship using the primary SEAL weapons: the M-16, SIG Sauer 9mm, and Colt .45. Heavy weapons use is also taught, including mastery of the M-60 machine gun and the M-79 and M-203 grenade launchers. Breath-hold diving to depths of 20 feet to place demolition charges is also a key element of this final phase of training. Attrition among students continues apace.

When BUD/S training is complete, the vast majority of students have rung out of the program. When Mark graduated in 1990, after 26 weeks of training, he was one of 19 remaining students from an original class of 121 men. He was named "Honorman," graduating first in his class. Students who complete BUD/S training are entitled to sport what SEALs call the "thousand-mile stare." It is the same stare Mark had seen on the face of Woody Woodruff the year before and on Jeff Schaeffer what seemed like a lifetime ago. But even with his well-earned stare in place, Mark's training was not yet complete. He went on to attend jump school at Fort Benning, Georgia, and then four more months of SEAL Qualification Training before being assigned to SEAL Team THREE's Alpha Platoon as assistant officer in charge, or AOIC.

Do You, Sandra, Take Cyborg . . .

In 1991, Mark began a series of deployments that took him around the world, to places like the Philippines, Iraq, Thailand, Malaysia, and South Korea. He was eventually promoted to platoon commander at SEAL Team THREE, then was later transferred to SEAL Delivery Vehicle Team ONE, a command that had him navigating small, wet submersibles launched from fast-attack submarines—and, in a sense, bringing him full circle, back to his youth on Lake Placid, dragged underwater by a motorboat. He saw men injured and had friends who were killed. Fortunately, the SEAL who was dragged to the bottom of the ocean was not one of them. The man had remembered his training, and, upon hitting the bottom at 50 feet, he took out his boot knife and calmly cut the rigging holding him to the magnet. Then he slowly swam to the surface. As his head bobbed up above the water, he shouted, "Here I am, Cy!" using Mark's nickname (it was short for "Cyborg," since it was widely held that he was half man, half machine). The SEAL had held his breath for three minutes.

Mark got married in 1994 to Sandra, who was from Coronado. But like many men before him, he very quickly found that the military and marriage were incompatible. His deployments didn't stop, and during their honeymoon in Hawaii he was called back to California for six weeks of training. Just three days after returning to his new bride, he was deployed to South Korea for six weeks. This pattern went on for over a year. In 1996, they had had enough. "I knew I had to make a choice between being married to Sandy and being married to the military," Mark recalled. "I had 7 years of service by that point, and of course the Navy tried very hard to convince me to stay in to get at least my 20 years and a retirement, but I chose to leave, and I made the right choice." He and Sandra adopted their son, Devon, who is now seven years old.

Once out of the Navy, Mark took a more entrepreneurial path, which was a challenging and often frustrating series of jobs that left him mostly unfulfilled. He started the Coronado Brewing Company, in partnership with his brothers-in-law, in 1996, using his business background to bring in investors and raise more than $1 million in financing. "I basically worked my butt off for three years, full-time, to get it off the ground," Mark said. "And it was successful. We were bringing in more than $2 million in revenue before I brought in someone else to run it." After some irreconcilable disagreements over how the business was being run and the direction to take it, he sold his interest to his brothers-in-law and moved on.

Getting His Feet Wet on the Web

A series of start-up efforts came next, none of which proved especially fulfilling. For a while, he worked as the CEO of a start-up software company called "Inasoft," in the process accumulating thousands of vested stock options. They all became worthless when the venture capitalists refused to continue funding the company, causing it to fold in 2003 before going public. He was a program director for a leadership institute and taught leadership skills at the University of San Diego, and he started a leadership training consultancy that had some large clients (including Starbucks). After 9/11, however, he and his partner decided to shutter this business because corporate clients immediately canceled events and put their training budgets on hold. As a member of the reserves, he was called back for a year of active duty after 9/11, and he spent time in Egypt, Kenya, and Bahrain. All the while, he sought a way to connect his passion for and commitment to the SEALs with his business background in a way that would make him happy and, of course, allow him to support his family.

The opportunity came in 2003. Mark had created an online community called NavySEALs.com a few years earlier, which he had hoped would become a virtual home for active-duty SEALs and reservists, as well as for civilians with an interest in the world of naval special operations. For several years it was little more than a placeholder, because he had neither the time nor the finances to support it. But after a redesign of the site in 2002, and perhaps as a result of the U.S. invasion of Iraq, the site began drawing lots of traffic and generating revenue. By late 2003, Mark finally had enough money to hire several people to help him manage the site as it grew. And then he was recalled for a second stint of active duty. This time, he would divide his time between Coronado and Iraq.

"The first recall, to Egypt, was voluntary, and I was only gone for three or four weeks at a time, which was OK with my wife," Mark said. "The second time, in January 2004, was involuntary." Mark was asked to prepare a report on an initiative for a division of the Marine Corps to join the Special Operations Command and also to develop a SEAL program called CERTEX. CERTEX (Certification Exercise) was the first effort to conduct a "capstone" exercise for SEAL teams before they deployed for combat. CERTEX was a period of intensive training through a highly complex series of war games. These war games were not canned exercises but rather dynamic missions that involved hundreds of role players (often in indigenous clothing) providing "intel" to SEAL units, intelligence that would then be synthesized and acted on (or not, since it might be phony) as operational demands required. Like the best role-playing games, CERTEX could take SEAL teams in various unscripted directions, forcing them to make command decisions that might compromise the mission or get them "killed." The intent was to create a fighting force with experience in "real" combat theaters—before arriving in one.

After a year, Mark's work with CERTEX, though unfinished, was so successful that the Navy once again asked him to return to active duty for another year. This time, he declined. But then he was approached with an appealing proposition. The Navy wanted to hire his leadership training company (now rebranded as U.S. Tactical) to continue working on the CERTEX program. It seemed a win-win. The Navy got what it wanted (essentially Mark, and his particularly unique set of skills), and Mark got a government contract to lead CERTEX, continuing involvement with the SEALs, and some spare time to continue development of NavySEALs.com as a community and e-commerce presence.

"The Web site is something I'm really passionate about," Mark said. "I have a lot of knowledge about this stuff, and a lot of experience, and I've basically become a Web recruiting arm for the SEALs," though he added that he is not compensated by the Navy for it. He also gives 7.5 percent of the site's profits to the Naval Special Warfare Foundation, a compensation fund for families of SEALs killed in the line of duty. "I'm finally at a point where I don't have to do anything else to support the site," Mark said. "I decided not to go out and get investors after my experience with the brewing company." With his Navy contract, he is doing scripting and scenario development for CERTEX and leading the event, which is a 10-day program twice a year, essentially a SEAL team's final "tune-up" before going off to war. U.S. Tactical was also recently hired by the Navy's Recruiting Command to bring retired SEALs into recruiting districts to help with the recruiting and mentoring of SEAL and Navy Diver candidates. The highly visible contract could, Mark hopes, help him realize his dream of having a significant positive impact on the future of the Navy SEAL program.

• • •

At one point toward the end of our conversations, I asked Mark if, after he had made his decision to become a SEAL, he had ever thought about being killed. He described a day, about 12 weeks into OCS, when he was eating a slice of pizza and watching television at a Newport, Rhode Island, restaurant. A news report came on the screen announcing that the United States had just invaded Panama in Operation Just Cause. Four SEALs, operating in an atypical multiplatoon group, had been killed in a firefight at Paitilla airfield. "I remember this as if it were yesterday, watching that and thinking 'These guys are just like me, they're just like me,'" Mark recalled. "I remember this sinking feeling, thinking that 'this isn't a video game I'm playing, this is real.'" But his mentor at the time, a SEAL officer candidate who had come up through the ranks and had been in Panama before the invasion, said to him, "If you're a warrior, there's no better honor than dying in combat. And you shouldn't be doing this if you don't have a warrior's spirit. And you do, or you wouldn't be here."

But what drives a man in pinstripes to become a warrior? It's a question I thought about often in my discussions with Mark. Obviously, he's not the first person to exchange a lucrative career for one with significantly less monetary reward and significantly more risk to life and limb. But on Wall Street, Mark was a fish out of water. Perhaps his warrior spirit drew him to his true occupation. The martial arts training at Seido Karate helped open his mind and intuition to this calling, and the SEALs offered a tantalizing package: a life spent in the water, a physically and emotionally demanding path, combined with the leadership training he sought and divorced from a life fixated on greed and materialism. For many fed up with the workaday world, it has an allure that's difficult to resist. When he left active duty, he was able to effectively combine his military experience and his business training to carve out a niche business, not one that's making him rich but one that's making him happy.

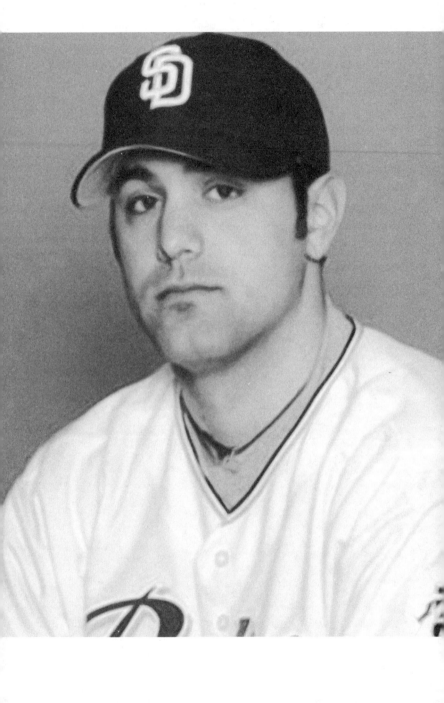

3

FREAKS, FLAMETHROWERS, AND PHENOMS

Life in the Minors

ESCAPE ARTIST: CHUCK BECHTEL
GREAT ESCAPE: FROM THE BULLPEN
TO THE MOUND

It's been said that the hardest thing in professional sports is to hit a pitched baseball. Funny, then, that baseball also appears to be the pro sport most accessible to the "common" person. Half of the guys out on the field, after all, wouldn't look out of place perched on a bar stool swigging beers. And, unlike other sports, baseball games feature a lot of standing around punctuated by occasional bouts of excitement. Who among us wouldn't like to earn millions swinging a bat, hanging out in the outfield, and eating sunflower seeds? But pitchers are a different breed altogether.

They don't look like Jackie Gleason. They're big, and they're tall, and they *work* for a living. And if hitting a pitched ball is the hardest thing in sports, then, well, throwing that ball 60 feet and 6 inches at 90 miles per hour and placing it within half an inch of where you want it must be a very close second.

The men who grow up to become professional baseball players have, nearly to a man, played organized baseball since they could pick up a bat and hit a ball off a "T." Playing pro ball is a kid's dream. But it's also a young man's game, and the older you get, the more your reflexes conspire to defeat you—and there's always another, younger man waiting to take your place. Still, if you're passionate about baseball, and you have the tools, you can't imagine doing anything else with your life. What does following that dream entail? It's a long, long drive, a literally endless road of 10-hour bus trips and dusty towns and sweaty ballparks and promotions and demotions and injury and surgery and rehab. It's years of chasing a dream that often seems just a few pitches away from becoming reality—or an injury away from becoming permanently out of reach.

But, if you can throw a baseball over the plate at 90 miles per hour, you may just get your shot at "the show." This is what a man passionate about baseball will do to get that shot.

These Hands Are Made for Milkin'

At six feet, four inches, and 220 pounds, Chuck Bechtel could have been a farm boy.

And, in fact, he might easily have been one. For seven decades his family owned a dairy farm in Royersford, Pennsylvania, about 30 miles west of Philadelphia. Looking at him, it's not difficult to imagine Chuck hauling a few dozen bottles of fresh cream to a delivery truck, perhaps with a cow thrown over each shoulder to cut down on the back-and-forth time.

Fortunately for Chuck—who had absolutely no interest in milking cows—his grandfather sold off the farm when Chuck was a kid. Also fortunately, Chuck discovered very early on that he could throw a baseball faster and with better accuracy than 99 percent of the population, so using his hands to pull an udder seemed akin to harnessing a thoroughbred to pull a milk wagon: He could probably do it, and do it quickly, but it wasn't exactly the best use of his talents.

• • •

Chuck was born in 1979, the third of three children, and the only boy. Back then, Royersford was a typical small farming town, a place where everyone knew everyone else and where Bechtel Dairy Farms, started by Chuck's great-grandfather, supplied the milk, cream, and butter to local businesses. But by the time Chuck was finishing grade school, the large supermarket chains had moved in and displaced most of the local suppliers, including the Bechtels. Chuck's father chose not to enter the family business, and instead he went to Kentucky to attend Union College. Eventually, the family ended up selling some of their land to the local high school so it could expand. Chuck's parents divorced when he was four, though his father continued to live in the area. But he credits his grandfathers along with his dad as being role models for him during his childhood. "I was very fortunate in that I had strong male role models in both my grandfathers, and I was very, very close to them." Both men lived nearby, and they came to virtually all of his games (baseball and basketball) growing up. "I don't think my Dad's dad missed any game I ever had."

Chuck's high school, Spring Ford, was an athletic powerhouse within its conference, which consisted mostly of other rural schools in southeastern Pennsylvania. But, particularly in basketball, when Chuck's team won its conference and went on to play other regional champions (including city schools such as the nationally ranked Chester High School), it got "crushed." "I was the center," Chuck said, "and I was matched up against guys who were 6-foot-10!" Though he did well in basketball, his real passion was always baseball: "I played basketball basically just to stay in shape for baseball," he admitted. I asked him how he did academically in high school. He paused before answering. "I'm one of those guys, . . . well, you hear people say that they could have done better if they had really wanted to? Any time that I really *tried* to do something academically, I did well, and I think I graduated with around a B+ average. I don't want to say it was easier for me . . ." Then he stopped and thought carefully about what he wanted to say. "I never had a job in high school," Chuck said. "I was told by my family, especially by my grandfather, that I should focus on school and sports. That's it. I wasn't allowed to have a job. All my friends were complaining about their jobs, and I was the only kid in my class who was saying 'I wish I could work!'"

"You Want to Do What?"

For Chuck, summer was all baseball, all the time. I wondered when he knew, or perhaps thought he knew, that he might try to make a career out of baseball. Though he is a modest man—he mentioned more than once that he didn't want to give the impression that he was "full of himself"—he always knew that he was "better than a lot of the guys I was playing against. And I remember I was in a meeting with my high school guidance counselor, and she asked me what I was going to do with my life—this was after I had gotten into college. And I told her I was going to play professional baseball. And she laughed, and then she asked, 'Well, what would you do if that didn't work out?' And I said, 'It's going to happen!'"

When he entered high school baseball, Chuck was put on the mound simply because he had a natural ability to throw harder than any of the other kids. Though, like most high school players, he had almost no formal coaching on the mechanics of throwing a baseball, by the time he graduated he was a "flamethrower," pitching regularly at 85 to 90 miles per hour—speeds more typical of college and professional baseball—with occasional pitches hitting the low 90s. He had a fastball and a curve, but typically he didn't even bother with his breaking pitch because he didn't have to: His fastball was so hard that most hitters were swinging too early and striking out.

Chuck was also an extraordinarily strong hitter. And it didn't hurt that most of the pitchers he faced were throwing in the 70s, which seemed like slow motion when he stood at the plate. In his senior year of high school, he was Pennsylvania MVP in summer league All Star ball, and his batting average was about .500. Ever modest, he noted that "not to take anything away from what I did, but the competition probably wasn't the greatest." Most of the pitchers he faced were "junkers" and "thumbers," guys who threw lots of off-speed pitches or who pitched "backwards in the count," throwing curveballs and change-ups when batters expected fastballs, hoping for strikeouts.

Chuck had decided that he wanted to attend a Division I college and that he wanted to start on the baseball team as a freshman. Several college scouts attended his high school and summer league games, hoping to convince him to commit. He eventually chose Marist College, a small Division I school in Poughkeepsie, New York, that offered him a "full ride," a completely paid-for education. But his success in high school and legion (summer league) baseball had brought scouts for the major leagues nosing around too. One day, toward the end of his last summer before starting college, he was approached by a scout for the Yankees. Might Chuck be interested, the man wanted to know, in signing with New York as a first baseman?

The Yankees Are Calling . . . Any Interest?

It's hard to overstate the difficulty—and the potentially life-changing consequences—of facing such a decision as a young person, someone who has yet to fully develop either as an athlete or as a mature adult. Scouts for pro teams (in all sports) dangle promises of money; expert coaching (something few high schoolers have experienced); and a fast track to stadiums filled with tens of thousands of cheering fans (not to mention groupies and assorted hangers-on). In effect, they promise and promote stardom to 17-year-olds of whom the vast majority will never make it out of minor league ball—if they even get that far. For Chuck, it was a tempting offer that, he said in retrospect, he was absolutely right to turn down in favor of going to college. "I know now that if I had signed with them as a first baseman, I would have been out of pro ball probably before my first season was over," he said. Why did he feel this way? "What some of those [young] guys can do, as a pitcher, the stuff they throw up there, is unbelievable. And the guys that can hit that stuff are even more incredible!"

On some level Chuck realized that, though he had experienced great success in high school, in a sense he had been a very big fish in a very small pond. The competition in other parts of the country, even at the high school level, was far beyond what he had been accustomed to seeing. "I didn't think that I was ready for pro ball yet—and I know now that I wasn't ready," Chuck said. "I wasn't ready for the lifestyle, and I wasn't ready for the competition. I had been facing guys who were throwing in the 70s and maybe, *maybe* 80, and then to face a guy throwing an 80-mile-per-hour *change-up*? When you haven't seen it before, going from somebody throwing 80 to somebody throwing 90 miles per hour, it looks like about a million." (Further, he noted that, as an 18-year-old out of a small town, he really wasn't ready to be sent away to, say, Eugene, Oregon, for a year, or more.)

I asked Chuck what accounted for this disparity in talent. How was it that one kid's pitches maxed out at 70 miles per hour while another kid, at the same age, could throw above 80 consistently? Were some kids better coached? Or were they bigger? Or stronger? Or did they simply pitch smarter? He said it was a combination of all three. "You can't really teach somebody to throw a baseball 90 miles per hour. That's simply a God-given talent. Some guys are just better athletically; they've been given different gifts." He went on, "Some guys can run a 6.3/60; some guys can hit 400-foot home runs with whatever you throw at them. And then there're the guys that don't have the kind of ability and talent that other guys have, but they're incredibly smart, and they know what to do and how to do it correctly. And those are the guys you don't like playing against, because those are the guys that are gonna beat you."

With his family, he decided he needed more time to prepare for the majors, and thus he declined the Yankees' offer. He began at Marist College in the fall of 1999.

* * *

Though Marist is a small liberal arts college in the Metro Atlantic Athletic Conference (MAAC)—and not a powerhouse especially known for athletic prowess—the year Chuck arrived coincided with a run of on-field successes unprecedented in the school's history. Starting in 1998, the school won four consecutive MAAC Commissioner's Cup trophies, awarded for overall excellence in 14 sports (both men's and women's); Marist was the first school in MAAC history to win four such trophies in a row. In particular, men's baseball was a standout: The team reached the National Collegiate Athletic Association (NCAA) regionals three years in a row, beginning in 2000, and in 2002 it broke numerous school records: 19 wins in a row, 41 wins overall, and the MAAC championship. That year saw three Marist baseball players, the most in the school's history, drafted by Major League Baseball.

Running Like a Fat Man, but a Cannon for an Arm

While being recruited in high school, Chuck had been told he would play first base for the Marist Red Foxes, which he did his first season. But one day after his freshman year, during summer baseball, a scout for the Detroit Tigers clocked him throwing 93 miles per hour across the diamond from first to third. Chuck recalled what the man said to him next: "He said, 'Well, let's see: You've got a cannon arm. You don't have the greatest hands, your feet aren't that quick, you've got a really long swing, and you run really slowly to first base, like a fat man. You need to concentrate on the mound.' So I said, okay then!" He added that some people—particularly athletes—don't like to be talked to that frankly, but he said that he's a realist:

"I'd rather somebody be completely blunt with me than be in limbo. I don't like being unaware."

Still, though he had the pitch speed, velocity was not enough. He needed better control of his pitches. "If you throw hard, [a scout] is going to come and see you pitch," Chuck noted. "But just because you throw hard doesn't mean you know how to pitch, and it doesn't mean you're going to get drafted." Fortunately, the coach of his summer league team, Joe Sottolano, happened to be the coach of Army's baseball team, and he had worked with many young pitching prospects in the past. He began his work with Chuck by first breaking down his mechanics and then, essentially, starting over. While he had a good fastball and a good curve, Chuck's fastball was "flat:" It traveled straight across the plate, with no movement. A flat fastball—unlike one that sinks in the zone—is the easiest pitch to hit, and though he had easily overcome high school players with his velocity, college ballplayers accustomed to seeing hard throwers would jump all over it. (He also pitched up in the strike zone, another minus.) "I had hideous mechanics when I went to college," Chuck recalled, "mostly because I had never had any formal instruction: I basically just went on the mound and threw." Eventually, everything changed: his grip on the ball, the position of the laces, his arm angle, and his wind-up.

After a summer of getting things right, starting at the beginning of his sophomore year at Marist, Chuck began practice as a pitcher. He continued relearning how to pitch, but he was soon confronted with the inevitable result of totally new mechanics: He had lost his velocity. Accustomed to throwing in the low 90s, he was now at 83 to 84 miles per hour. For a pitcher accustomed to overpowering hitters and blowing pitches by them, it was a painful setback. "Needless to say, I was really frustrated!" Chuck recalled. "But he kept saying, 'Stick with it, keep working at it, you're going to get used to it, and your velocity's going to come back.'" Through the fall and into the winter of his sophomore year, he practiced. Adding to the pressure to perform was the fact that in college baseball, sophomore year is the critical make-or-break season for young prospects. Have a good year and the scouts will hear about it, begin coming to games, and start talking about the draft the following season. Have a bad year and, well, it could be time to start thinking about life without professional baseball.

When the season began in the spring, it was clear that all Chuck's hard work had paid off. He was back throwing in the low 90s, topping out at a blistering 95 miles per hour, putting movement on the ball, throwing strikes, and—most important—getting guys out. It appeared that he was on his way.

Then he blew out his elbow.

A Lost Season

There are three things that determine how far a young athlete trying to make it to the pros can progress: talent, the open positions on professional teams, and injury. Fortunately, medical advances—particularly in arthroscopic surgery—over the last 20 years have meant that injuries that once might have been career ending are now treatable. The problems associated with recovery, however, continue. Professional baseball is primarily a young man's game, and missing months (or a full season) of play not only throws off timing and conditioning but it also means an opportunity for a younger player with talent to take your place. And, particularly in college ball, it can mean delaying a year of eligibility for the draft.

The doctors told Chuck the tendons in his elbow looked like spaghetti: Everything was stretched out and worn down, not from poor mechanics (though that probably didn't help) but because he had thrown too many pitches while playing in high school. Though he was assured that his arm would recover and he would be able to pitch again, it was a scary time. "It was a reality check," Chuck remembered. "I had been floating a bit on Cloud 9, and I guess I kind of had tunnel vision, just thinking baseball, baseball, baseball all the time. And then when I blew out my elbow, I realized that I had better concentrate on my schooling. Just in case."

As it always seems to, injury had come at the worst possible time. Before he got hurt during sophomore year, Chuck was having a season that college pitching prospects dream about. He was the No. 1 starter on his team, with a record of 5–0 and an earned run average (ERA) of 1.5, putting him fourth in the nation in ERA. He was being scouted heavily, and he was scheduled to play summer ball with the Cotuit Kettleers of the Cape Cod Baseball League, the most competitive and prestigious amateur college league in the nation. But now his sophomore season was officially over. Chuck had elbow surgery in May 2000, and he did not play the entire summer—the first time he had missed a summer of baseball since he had played T-ball as a five-year-old.

Chuck was officially a junior in the fall of 2000, and junior year for student athletes is the all-important "eligibility year," the year they are eligible for the professional draft. But because of his surgery, Chuck "redshirted" in the spring of 2001, opting not to play to give his arm time to recover. By redshirting, he skipped the 2001 season and gave himself two more years of eligibility for the draft. His first season back, in spring of 2002, was one of readjustment, and he didn't have a great year. He finished with a respectable record of 8 and 4, but he was hobbled by the pitcher's greatest foe: inconsistency. His velocity was up, and then it was down. His control wavered. He clearly did not have the same stuff. Chuck recalled it as a trying time, one filled with some success but also doubt. "I used to play it over and over in my mind: What if? What if I hadn't gotten hurt," he said. Still, he knew that recovery from injury and surgery was a process, one not unlike the setbacks he had faced after changing his pitching mechanics two years before.

Perhaps surprisingly, he got drafted anyway. The San Diego Padres had been scouting Chuck prior to his injury, and they were not dissuaded by his middling season. Apparently the team was confident that he had enough talent to work his way back to where he had been. He was offered a very modest signing bonus of $1,000 and money to pay for the rest of his schooling (he had a few credits left to earn, but the offer of payment was a moot point, since he was attending on a scholarship anyway).

The Draft

The college draft is a complex, highly competitive, and secretive spectacle in which often-empty promises and money are tossed about in equal measures, an event where student athletes—some not yet old enough to drink—are offered millions of dollars in guaranteed money (called "signing bonuses") if they agree to sign their professional lives away to the highest bidder. Hovering around the margins of the draft are a phalanx of family members, coaches, managers, lawyers, agents, fellow athletes, "friends," and the media—and anyone else with a potential interest (monetary or otherwise) in professional athletes. Behind the curtain and away from the lights are the hard questions athletes must ask themselves before making their decisions. Should I finish school and get my degree, or should I go pro? What if I get injured? Might I get a better offer from another team next year? What if I don't get my degree, and then I get injured? What will I do with my life then? Like Chuck, virtually all potential draftees have spent their lives playing sports, with perhaps minimal thought to what might come next.

Getting drafted meant that, regardless of whether he signed with the team, Chuck's rights were held by the Padres for a year. He could not sign with any other team until the next draft the following June, at which time San Diego could make another (hopefully better) offer, or Chuck would be released and free to sign with another club. In one sense, the low cash offer was a bit of unintended luck. It made the team's offer that much easier to decline; one could be seriously tempted by tens or hundreds of thousands of dollars, but a thousand bucks was little more than a token dispensation. Chuck took pains to make it clear that the Padres' offer was less than appealing even aside from the small signing bonus. "It wasn't so much the money; it was more that I wanted to finish my degree. Plus I knew I could pitch better, and I wanted an opportunity to raise my stock."

For the second time in his brief career, Chuck passed on the chance to enter Major League Baseball.

.   .   .

Throughout the following summer and into the winter, Chuck worked on improving his control even though, at times, his elbow hurt, his arm was killing him, and his velocity was down. Again, he had to relearn how to pitch. Making things even more difficult, all the players in his original class had graduated, and he missed the camaraderie they had shared over four years with the Marist team. And, further, younger guys had joined the team, and some of them had better stuff than he did, putting added pressure on him to perform or lose his spot in the rotation. I asked Chuck if, up to this point, he had given any serious thought about what might happen if a career in baseball didn't work out. He had managed a B average at Marist, even while devoting most of his time to baseball, and he had majored in criminal justice. Interestingly, he mentioned the appeal of firefighting. "My roommate freshman year disappeared one morning, and when he came back four hours later, he said he had taken his FDNY fire test." Chuck was intrigued. Coming from a small town where firefighters were all volunteers, he hadn't given much thought to the fact that it might be a career too and one that could support a family. "It sparked an interest," Chuck said. "And anyway it's always good to have a backup plan, in case things don't work out."

The Padres Return. Twice.

And then suddenly, one day a few weeks into his final season, it all came back. "I know it sounds crazy, but I showed up one day for practice, and everything just clicked," Chuck recalled. "I went into practice, and I got into the cage with the hitters, and I was throwing 90 to 93 miles per hour. My velocity was back, I had control, and I was getting guys out. My fifth year was a lot of fun because it was a lot of success." That year, 2003, Chuck threw the first nine-inning no-hitter in Marist history, his ERA was under 2 runs per game, he was named national pitcher of the week, and he was pitcher of the year in his conference. The Padres took notice, this time offering him a $15,000 signing bonus just before the draft began. Now working with a sports agent who had come recommended by a fellow player, Chuck sat down and took serious stock of what he might be worth to another Major League team. His agent told him that, if he declined the Padres' offer, he would most likely "fall" (be chosen) in the first 10 rounds—possibly the first 8—by another ball club. (The Major League draft has 50 rounds.) After all, he had just completed his best season ever, with the honors to prove it. But going this route was clearly a gamble. Chuck was turning down guaranteed cash on the table in the hope of getting not only another offer, but a better one. On the other hand, if in fact he *was* taken in the early rounds, he would almost certainly get more than a $15,000 signing bonus—and possibly much, much more.

Unfortunately, the bet didn't pay off. Watching the draft on television, Chuck was a bundle of nervous energy as round after round went by and he did not fall. Ten rounds. Twelve rounds. Fourteen. Finally, Chuck's phone rang during the fifteenth round. His agent told him he had been chosen—a big, big plus. He was relieved. But then came the bad news: He had been selected by, of all teams, the Padres. Now they had him over a barrel, and his choices were not great. If he declined the Padres' offer, they would again hold his rights for a year, eliminating any opportunity for Chuck to play for another team until the following draft. But now, they didn't have to offer him $15,000, because they knew he wouldn't be able to jump to another club. He accepted a reduced offer, and, after a long and arduous road, Chuck had finally realized his dream: He was now officially a professional baseball player, part of the San Diego Padres' farm system.

But the minor leagues would prove to be a long, long way from "the show."

Freaks and Phenoms: Life in the Minors

The minor leagues of Major League Baseball are a baseball universe unto themselves, with their own distinct cities (or towns, as the case may be), geographic leagues, teams, coaches, staffs, umpires, and ballparks. Each major league team has a farm system that itself has multiple teams, and each team represents a rung on the ladder that eventually—if you're talented, lucky, and healthy—leads to the majors. The levels themselves are a complex hierarchy with differing goals, but the basic structure, in ascending order, is as follows: Rookie ball, Short-Season A ball, Low A ball (A–), High A ball (A+), AA (called "double A"), AAA ("triple A"), and "the bigs." The boundaries between the levels can be fluid, and players move in both directions, depending on their age, ability, experience, and health (injured major leaguers are often "sent down" to recuperate in the less intensive, less media-saturated environment of the minors). Four things are common to all levels of the minor leagues: The ballparks are small, the pay is minimal, and the travel is by bus. And you have to lug your own gear.

Chuck was initially sent to Short-Season A in Eugene, Oregon. (He skipped Rookie ball, which is typically for players signed just out of high school.) After only a week and a half, he was moved up to Low A ball, to the Fort Wayne (Indiana) Wizards, the San Diego affiliate in the Midwest League. He did well, though he found the competition, naturally, to be more skilled than he was used to. For the first time, he also began playing against true major league prospects, the players who had been standouts even among stars in college. "Every now and then you'd run into a guy who was a prospect, and it was as if they were freaks: They could just do stuff. I mean, some of the stuff I'd seen guys do was unbelievable," he recalled. "Plays where you think there is not a *shot* that somebody would even come *close* to getting the ball, and they make it look really easy. How fast some guys are, how far guys can hit a ball, how hard they can throw it with accuracy. It's just unbelievable."

But while he enjoyed playing, the life itself was hard. The travel was constant, and it wasn't comfortable. The slightly more senior players would have two seats on the bus to themselves, while the younger guys (most of them over six feet—and sometimes, like Chuck, well over) were forced to double up on 10-hour bus trips to distant towns. Sometimes, depending on the arrangement the team had, players would live with host families. Other teams might put all the players up in an apartment complex. Most of the players in Low and High A ball fell into the same general age group, from about 19 to 23. I noted to Chuck that it almost sounded like going into basic training, and he agreed. "You're going into an atmosphere with a bunch of guys who you don't know," Chuck said. "But, depending on how well you get along with others, you do start to form friendships and camaraderie with the rest of the team."

Like the Army, there was also a lot of waiting: for games, to be put into games, for buses, on buses. On the bus, players had various strategies to combat the boredom. Guys would read, or watch movies, or sleep, or just stare out the window. Though the games themselves could be exciting, much of the enjoyment depended on the local market and the draw of the minor league team. "Some places, we'd get 10,000 people; other places, we'd get 100," Chuck said. "And it makes a difference in the enthusiasm of the game. There'd be some places where we'd show up, and it's boring, and it's hot, it's a crappy town, and it's just not fun." The crowds also played a role in how motivated the players were. That shouldn't have mattered, though, because, as Chuck pointed out, good players should be able to motivate themselves for every game regardless of its circumstances. Nevertheless, with 140 games in a minor league season, some games were much more work than play.

Money? What Money?

And, of course, there were the miserably low salaries. In 2006, the minimum salary in Major League Baseball (the big leagues) was $327,000. (But the average salary probably better reflects true pay across the league. In 2006 it was about $2.8 million, according to published reports.) Minor leaguers, on the other hand, receive less than $1,000 per month during their first contract season, plus a meal allowance, for road games only, of $20. Even AAA players—those at the top level of the minors—typically make less than $30,000 per year, though just one day played in the majors can bump the salary above $50,000. Fortunately, health insurance is included for those on the roster.

What hangs over the minors like a dark cloud and that typically remains little discussed among players is that the great enemy is time. As the years pass and players age, their chances of being called up to the show go down commensurately. "Old" is a relative term, of course, but major league teams tend to like their players as young as possible—directly out of high school is preferable. Bringing players in young allows teams to mold and shape them to fill whatever role they feel is appropriate.

And it means there's less time wasted on having to relearn (or unlearn, as Chuck had to do) how to do things: throw, pitch, hit, and run. Further, as the players age, their reflexes slow down, putting them at a competitive disadvantage when compared to newer blood. As minor league players get older, there's almost no margin for error, no room for a long streak of bad pitching or a poor season.

After his first season in the minors, Chuck returned for spring training in 2004. Everyone he had played with had been moved up to High A ball, but he found out that he would not be moving on. Some of the reason for this decision was roster related, because the High A team (the Lake Elsinore Storm) didn't need another right-handed pitcher. But he was also told that he needed to work on his control. He had been pitching as a middle reliever, called into close games in the middle innings for what were typically short stretches of work (one or two innings) to get batters out and keep the score close. While this role required fewer pitches than work as a starter, there was little room for error, and mistakes were greatly magnified. A few hits by the opposing team, or a few walks, and a close game could be knocked out of reach. Chuck's ERA was under 2, but the organization felt he needed more pitching experience before moving up. Needless to say, he was disappointed. "I was expecting to be moved up," he said. And not only that. He was 24 years old—clearly not "old" in any realm outside professional sports, but at the older end of the Low A age range. Fortunately, the setback was temporary, and in the middle of the 2004 season, he was moved up to Lake Elsinore.

Prospects and Problems

In June of 2004, however, things began to change. Chuck had done well, but apparently not well enough. A young right-handed pitcher, a hard-throwing prospect who had been drafted in the early rounds, was doing very well and began to move up in the Padres' organization. Chuck found himself in an unenviable position common to many players in the minors. He was in his midtwenties, not yet in AA or AAA ball, and all of a sudden he was competing for a roster spot with a young phenom in whom the team had already invested a significant sum. Chuck was moved back down to Low A, and just like that, it seemed the writing was on the wall. "Everything just kind of fell through right there," Chuck remembered. "I was a little upset, but also I just started pitching badly. I was getting hit." He didn't speculate about whether his disappointment about his demotion affected his pitching, but it clearly didn't help his confidence. With just a few weeks left in the 2004 season, Chuck finally got the call. The Padres were releasing him.

• • •

The next few months were a series of peaks and valleys. Just days after being released by the Padres, Chuck was picked up by the Detroit Tigers' organization and sent to the Florida State League, playing High A ball. But his midseason contract was not renewed, and he was again a free agent. In 2005 he signed with St. Louis, for $1,400 per month, again playing High A. He pitched for several months, but his shoulder began giving him trouble, and he was placed on the disabled list (DL). By the time he came off the DL, Chuck felt the end was near. His control had been suffering, and he wasn't getting batters out. Moreover, the draft was approaching, with a new crop of younger players coming in, and the team could not afford to keep him on the roster. He had a meeting with the coach. "I saw it coming," Chuck recalled. "We didn't part on bad terms, but the coach was saying, 'Listen, you're 25 years old, we were expecting you to be in AA by now, but you got hurt, and we don't have any room for you.' And I knew it. I understood. So I thanked him for the opportunity to play."

Then he walked out the door.

The Last Stop

Both ballparks are virtually brand new, and both were built in the fashion currently in vogue among designers of urban ballparks, the by now well-worn "it's-a-new-stadium-but-it-has-bricks-not-concrete-on-the-outside-to-make-it-look-like-it-could-be-old-even-though-everyone-knows-it's-state-of-the-art" concept. Both parks have a great view of the Delaware River, and both sit about a mile from downtown Philadelphia. Both are easily accessible by car, and naturally both are surrounded by acres of parking lots. And both are home to baseball clubs that tend to entertain fans while finishing with so-so records and no championships. That's where the similarities end.

One ballpark is Citizens Bank Park, home of the Philadelphia Phillies and located just south of downtown Philadelphia.

The other is Campbell's Field, home of the Atlantic League's Camden Riversharks, across the Delaware River in Camden, New Jersey—and separated from Major League Baseball by much, much more than a half mile of brackish northeast waterway.

The Atlantic League of Professional Baseball is one of a number of independent—that is, unaffiliated with the majors—baseball leagues around the country. The Atlantic is a full-season league (140 games) with eight teams based in various cities and towns in Pennsylvania (Lancaster, York); New Jersey (Camden, Somerset, Newark); New York (Long Island); and Connecticut (Bridgeport). Conceived just after the MLB's disastrous strike season of 1994 to 1995, the Atlantic League began operations in 1998 as an East Coast alternative to affiliated baseball, and teams are usually based in areas underserved by the majors and minors. Ballparks are small (typically 5,000 to 7,000 seats), ticket prices are low, parking is practically free, and families in particular are courted with everything from carousels to rock-climbing walls to potato-sack races between innings. Sno Cones are three bucks.

Players arrive at the Atlantic League at various ages and with varying experience in the major league farm system; most have spent at least a few years in the minors and some have even played in the show. Though MLB scouts attend Atlantic League games and a talented few of the league's top players move up to the majors, typically the trajectory is in the other direction. (The league seeks to court players with, on average, six years in the minor league system, and there were more than 600 such players in 2005.) For some guys, the league is simply a way to continue to be paid (albeit minimally) to play the sport they love, one they've been playing virtually their entire lives. For others, it's a final shot, a chance to show what they can do on the field. In essence, it's an opportunity to be seen and hopefully to be called up. Games are usually played at a fairly high level, and they can be just as exciting as major league games—often more so because the ballparks are so intimate. An average Atlantic League game may have a few more errors, a few more pitchers with control problems, and a few less home runs than its MLB equivalent. But with field box seats just $10, most fans seem not to notice, or care. Besides, where else can you find an evening of entertainment featuring not only some pretty decent baseball but also a shopping cart derby, two kids racing around the infield holding giant plastic toothbrushes, and tykes dropping colored balls into plastic buckets in a modified version of "Hungry Hungry Hippos"?

Halfway through the 2005 season, now without a ball club, Chuck called a friend who was playing for the Camden Riversharks. The friend arranged a meeting with Steve Foucault, the team's pitching coach, who liked what he saw in Chuck's pitching, though with some reservations. "You see guys, and you wonder why they haven't gotten more of an opportunity to progress through the upper levels of the minors," said Foucault, a bearish man with a drooping moustache who pitched in the majors through much of the 1970s. "Chuck has never gotten the opportunity to pitch much above A ball, and the problem he had was more of a control problem, with his fastball, and not being able to throw his breaking ball over the plate for a strike. He was trying to throw his fastball every time at 100 percent velocity, and it's just very difficult to do that," Foucault said. "And I told him, 'If you can throw at 95, then you need to pitch around 91 to 92, and then when you need a strikeout, when the guy's got two strikes, you can throw at 95, and there's enough on it to get the strikeout. But until you need to do that, until you get those two strikes, there's no need to throw the ball as hard as you can.'" He added that, at 27 or 28 and with no experience playing AA or AAA ball, chances are that a pitcher isn't likely to get another opportunity. "But, you never know," Foucault added. "It has happened."

Chuck arrived at Camden midseason in 2005. He was a new face on the bench, but overall the drill was a familiar one. Like the minors, daily life in the Atlantic League can be a grind, with games virtually every day of the summer and often sparse crowds. Travel was by bus, though the farthest the team had to travel was about three hours, to Bridgeport. The critical difference between the two leagues, of course, is that the minor leagues lead to the majors, while the Atlantic League leads to the minors; it's an additional step on what can be a long and frustrating climb.

A Long, Hot Summer

Campbell's Field, home of the Riversharks, was actually built by Rutgers University on the Camden New Jersey waterfront, on a site occupied for a century by the Campbell's Soup Company. The drive from Philadelphia to the ballpark takes you east across the scenic Benjamin Franklin Bridge (the longest suspension bridge in the world when it opened in 1926) and then slightly south. Camden itself feels like an odd place for a sparkling new stadium on the water. It is a gritty, impoverished place tainted by a history of political corruption, and it perpetually tops federal rankings of the country's most dangerous cities. But the ballpark is on the edge of town, and the stands face north and west, away from Camden, affording marvelous views of the water, the light blue-painted steel of the bridge, and the Philadelphia skyline.

After he left affiliated baseball and joined an independent league, Chuck's agent stopped returning his phone calls—a situation not uncommon for younger players not signed for big bonuses in the early rounds of the draft. But Chuck kept a positive attitude, and he had a decent half season as a middle reliever with the Riversharks in 2005, typically called in any time after the sixth inning to shut opponents down. He finished with a record of 1 and 0 and a so-so ERA of 5.05. The team did well, finishing at 80 and 60, tied for the top record in the league. However, the 'Sharks collapsed in September, going 10 and 13 and missing the playoffs. (It wasn't all bad news for the organization, however. Chris Widger, a former Riversharks catcher, became the only player in team history to make it to a major league roster: He played backup catcher on the Chicago White Sox, which won the 2005 World Series. Still, he was the exception that proved the rule: The odds of making it to the show from the Atlantic League were long indeed.)

The ball club re-signed Chuck for the 2006 season. When we met and I began watching him pitch early in the year, the team had a losing record and sat at the bottom of the Atlantic

League's South Division, 8 games behind the first-place Lancaster Barnstormers. But the wins came more easily as the spring progressed, and by June, Chuck's record looked promising: He had appeared in 11 games, pitching about 13 total innings, and he had given up just two earned runs. He also had eight strikeouts, and his ERA was a very respectable 1.35.

The problem, once again, was his consistency, and a string of games in late May and early June were illustrative. In an away game against the Newark Bears, Chuck was given the nod to pitch two innings of relief in a game the Riversharks were leading 5 to 0. He struck out three and did not allow a hit. A few days later, in a home game against the Somerset Patriots, Chuck came in and again pitched two strong innings of relief, allowing no hits, striking out one, and helping the team secure an 8 to 4 victory. But two days later, with the Riversharks leading the Patriots 6 to 0, Chuck took the mound in the top of the seventh to try to shut the Patriots down. Things got messy in a hurry.

After giving up a lead-off double, Chuck gave up a drop-in single to left, and a run scored. The third batter stroked a single up the right field line, and all of a sudden the Patriots had runners at first and third with nobody out. Clearly frustrated, Chuck threw a wild pitch, and the runner at first base advanced. Finally, the next batter hit a grounder to third and was thrown out at first. But the next batter, after running the count to 3 and 2, hit another grounder to third, and another run crossed the plate. It was now 6 to 2. At this point, pitching coach Steve Foucault walked over to the mound, and the two had a brief conversation. Chuck got the final out of the inning with a ground ball to first, but his night was over. He had pitched just one inning—giving up three hits, tossing a wild pitch, and allowing two earned runs. Baseball is a game of momentum, and in the ballpark the feeling that the momentum had shifted to the Patriots during Chuck's brief appearance was almost palpable. Somerset added three more runs in the top of the eighth, and just like that, a 6 to 0 drubbing had become a one-run game. The Riversharks went on to win, but only just, by a final score of 8 to 6. Oddly, Chuck's pitch placement seemed good—wild pitch notwithstanding—and he had decent velocity. But, as he noted to me later, sometimes you throw well, and you get hit; other times, "You couldn't hit the side of a barn if you were standing right in front of it, and you get guys out!"

As the saying goes, it's a long season, and this is especially true for low-paid players not yet in the majors. A player's bat gets hot, winning teams cool off, and streaks begin and end every day. Like the Riversharks, Chuck has had bad days amidst flashes of brilliance, but there's no denying he's an exciting pitcher to watch. Few pitchers, even in the majors, are able to throw a baseball at 93 miles an hour, much less over the plate. And, as a fan, if the price you have to pay to see such remarkable skill is an occasional wild pitch, a few walks, or a blowout that turns into a squeaker, well, that's part of baseball's allure.

The big question, of course, is whether Chuck has enough time left to achieve his dream, to do the only thing he's wanted to do since he was old enough to swing a bat. How much more time does he give himself? As he said early in our first meeting, he's a realist and likes to see and hear things as they are. With plans to get married in the fall, he was quick to point out that he can't support a family on his current salary of $1,500 a month. He's nearly 27, and any pitching scout would tell him, rightly, that in baseball years he's old, particularly since he's never played above single A ball. In a moment of frank introspection, he admitted that this season may be his last, assuming he does not get the call.

But might not a scout attend a Camden Riversharks game, spot him throwing, and call him up, at least to the minors? It's possible, certainly, though not probable. Scouts for the majors typically look to bring players up just after the All Star break in July, and then at the end of the season, when major league teams are making their playoff runs. But not only would Chuck need to be seen—and, naturally, be pitching well—but a potential big league team would also have to require the services of a right-handed middle reliever. And there's rarely a shortage.

Chuck realizes his window is closing. But he is far from angry. He plays because he loves the game, and he loves to compete. "I was given the opportunity to do something that little boys dream of, to grow up and become a baseball player. And I've had a lot of fun with it so far," he said. "But I can't . . ." He trailed off before continuing. "You can let something be a dream for only so long, and then you have to leave it at that. As a dream."

Not long ago, Chuck took the qualification exam for eligibility to become a Philadelphia firefighter. He thinks of it as a backup plan, a safely blanket. But the job also has a particular type of appeal. "I like being that guy in relief they go to when they need to get people out. And as a firefighter, I want to be the guy they put the responsibility on when they need to get someone out of a building. I guess I like being the one they go to when they need to get something done."

Nearing the end of our conversations, he pondered what life might be like without baseball. He may continue to teach pitching or coach kids, as he does in the off-season. But whatever he ends up doing, he knows he wants it to be something active. "I need to be doing something that's physically demanding," he said. "As a firefighter, you're still a member of a team, and you have people counting on you. And I like that," Chuck noted finally. "If I had to sit in a cubicle all day, I would kill myself."

4

EXTREME ENTREPRENEURSHIP

ESCAPE ARTIST: DAN EGAN

GREAT ESCAPE: FROM A STORM AT 18,000 FEET

Extreme athletes have always taken outsized risks to pursue the sports they love: What makes their sports "extreme" if not that rush of danger? But while today's talented extreme skiers, like their counterparts in other extreme sports, have enough media exposure to make a living, this wasn't the case in the early years of the "extreme sports" movement. The vast majority of those men (and, occasionally, women) did it for fun, not profit. If they made enough to travel and avoid a "real job," then that was enough.

A few smart and talented people, however, were slightly ahead of the curve, and these athletes had the foresight to understand the importance the media (particularly film and television) would play in moving extreme athletics into the mainstream. Dan Egan is one of those people. He figured out a way to craft a business from the sport he loved, and though he never got rich—and was only a tiny bit famous in extreme skiing's earliest inner circle—he had vision. In combining his passion for skiing with an entrepreneurial spirit, he paved the way for the generation of media-savvy athletes who would follow.

And he didn't let minor things like almost freezing to death on the side of a Russian mountain hold him back.

The Elbrus Descent

Dan Egan knew he was probably going to die.

He wasn't prepared for death, exactly. He was only 26. But he accepted that it was a relative certainty.

How else to account for the bright light? How else to explain his vision in this desolate place, a mental image of a field full of workers, beckoning him, offering to lead him, to show him the way?

At altitude, he knew, the mind plays tricks on the body, and the body responds slowly to the brain's commands. Thinking clearly in thin air is not possible; it's as if the brain is lost in a fog that can't be penetrated and never clears, as if every thought is slowed to each of its component parts. Walking down the steep, snow-covered slope consisted of excruciating, slow-motion achievements. Lift right leg. Transfer weight to left foot. Move right leg forward one pace. Rest. Progress was measured not in time, or meters, or even feet. It was a battle for inches. A game of baby steps. They had made it to the summit. But now they needed to get back down. On their own. No rescue team would be ascending to lend assistance. No helicopter would fly to this altitude. Not in this weather, not for days.

But Dan also knew that staying put might be even worse. The team might be buried alive. Or die of thirst. Or freeze to death. Perhaps he was already freezing to death. Maybe this was how it felt.

Without warning, a storm had blown up the mountain from below, dropping more than five feet of snow on Mount Elbrus, in the Caucasus Main Range in Russia. Few people outside the insular worlds of extreme skiing and mountaineering had even heard of Elbrus—though at 18,513 feet it was the highest point in Europe. Like all high peaks, the weather on Elbrus swung from extremes virtually without warning. Though Dan and his group had set out from base camp in moderate conditions (some wind, light snow), things had deteriorated rapidly. They had made the summit—a few of them, anyway—but getting down had proved impossible. He had now been lost for the better part of a day, without food, and without water. Visibility was zero, mocking the video camera he had taken to document the trip. But his regrets about the equipment were incidental. He was more worried about his older brother, John, who had accompanied him on the trip. During the ascent, they had decided to split up into two groups, and John had gone with the other group of skiers. They had been some ways behind, and Dan wondered if John had made it off the mountain. He prayed his brother had been able to turn back and reach base camp before the storm hit.

But he wasn't confident. He was scared.

And he was sure he was freezing to death. He vaguely understood, somewhere in the back of his mind, that he had just hours left. Huddled and shivering in the shallow snow shelter he had carved from the powder, he thought ruefully of the great slogan he had dreamed up a year before, the marketing pitch he and John had used when they tried to woo sponsors. Still in its infancy in 1990, extreme skiing was on the periphery, a sport with few fans and no money, a sport still searching for the cachet that would come with the creation of the X Games and the Gravity Games a few years later. But Dan had always seen a business opportunity there, and every business, he knew, needed a great pitchman. Or pitchmen. So the brothers had come up with a slogan, a tag line that both mocked the relative obscurity of extreme skiing and placed the brothers at its forefront.

"Haven't you heard of us?" the line went. "We're the Egan Brothers." Strategic pause. "From Vermont!" They were really from Boston, but no matter. That wasn't the point. The point was to create a branded image in a sport that had no real commodities, no stars. "The Egan Brothers" was a catchphrase, something to remember.

And, indeed, it seemed now that Dan and John would get their wish. With finality, Dan realized, they would never be marketed as "The Egan Brothers, from Vermont!" They would be memorialized: The Egan Brothers. From Mount Elbrus.

He's No Hippie, He's My Brother

Dan Egan grew up in Boston, the fifth of seven children, five boys and two girls. The son of a doctor father and a mother who was "a saint" (what else would you call a woman who raises seven kids?). Dan came from a family that bred and fostered both competition and independence. And most of both were manifested in freestyle skiing and downhill racing.

Now 41, in the late 1970s Dan was just 13 when he watched his older brother John forgo college to join the professional ski racing circuit. But it was somewhat less glamorous than that: "Basically, he became a ski bum," Dan recalled. "He skied during the day and washed dishes at night." Though he watched as John struggled financially, Dan also saw—in the typical way that kids view adults who take nontraditional career paths—that such a trajectory could be fun, for a time. "I wouldn't say that John hung around with hippies—this was the late 1970s—but more what hippies had become," Dan said. "It was just a hodgepodge of characters, doing their own thing, kids who saw themselves as unconventional." Though few had anything more than a high school education, most of his brother's friends managed to get by as best they could (by legitimate means or not), all joined by a love of skiing, primarily at Sugarbush in Vermont. While John had some success ski racing, he was not making a living.

Not surprisingly, Dan's parents took a somewhat dimmer view of his brother's lifestyle, which included, at various times, the stereotypical "living out of a van." And, of course, they were "not too happy" about their 13-year-old son tagging along with his brother's gang. But for Dan, it was a life that spoke to him on many levels, a life focused on sport, on the outdoors, and perhaps above all on a more flexible way of living.

The Salad Days

Dan grew into an accomplished athlete in high school, and he was recruited for soccer by Babson College in Wellesley, Massachusetts. Though he liked school, he described himself as "not a great student." But at Babson, he discovered the flexibility he had been seeking. Instead of staying in school fall, winter, and spring (like everyone else), he took his winter semesters off so that he could ski. He then made up his missed credits in the summers. And, in fact, he was, if not encouraged, then at least tacitly supported by the school staff. "They basically told me that as long as I could keep up, I could go when I wanted," he remembered. Perhaps not coincidentally, at the time Babson—already with a reputation as a solid business school—was gaining notoriety for its program in entrepreneurship, still a relative novelty in the early 1980s. (In 2005, Babson's MBA program was ranked No. 1 by *U.S. News & World Report* and No. 2 by the *Wall Street Journal*.) He began to take the classes that would play a major role in his career decisions later on. "I learned that it was possible to take your passion, whatever it was, and find a path to success," Dan said. It was a lesson he would never forget.

In the spring of 1986, still with a year left at Babson, he found himself working part-time as the night check-in manager at a hotel in Sugarbush to make a little extra cash—not exactly the first step of an entrepreneurial path to riches. After scraping together enough money, he bought a one-way ticket to California (People's Express, $75) and then hitched a ride to Lake Tahoe. Skiing all day long, he practiced his cliff jumping, often launching off cornices high above the tree line and watching as rocky cliffs raced by under his skis before he landed in deep powder.

Financially strapped (lift tickets, then as now, were expensive), he ate judiciously and creatively. One strategy involved hitting "as many of the two-for-one après-ski parties as I could find!" he laughed. Once tired of California, he thumbed his way to Denver, with his skis strapped to his back. It was at Aspen that winter that he began to see new possibilities in a skiing career.

In the winter of 1986, Aspen hosted the Pro Mobile Freestyle Tour, sponsored by Coors beer. Though entrance fees were high, the tournament was winner take all; and if he won, he would be looking at thousands in prize money—and the possibility of endorsement deals. In December 1987, Dan convinced his brother to come out of "retirement" and enter the contest, to be held at Aspen and Vail that year. There was only one problem: Neither of them had money for a plane ticket. Coincidentally, the New England Patriots were scheduled to play the Denver Broncos in an AFC Divisional Playoff game on January 4. Their friend Stan had tickets for the game and was flying out. Would Stan be willing to let the brothers drive his Jeep to Denver? Sure, Stan said, no problem; he'd drive it home after the game. John and Dan drove the car out but then conveniently "forgot" to deliver it to Stan. (To make matters worse, the Pats lost, and the brothers crashed the car.)

Dan and John entered the "Friday Bump Contest" at Aspen, and though they didn't win, they put themselves on the freestyle skiing map. "The Egan Brothers from Vermont," as they incessantly referred to themselves, had arrived. After Dan finished at Babson in the spring of 1987, he and John joined the 1988 World Pro Mogul Tour in Vail, where Dan made it to the round of 16, bringing in a cash prize of a few hundred dollars. They decided to stay out west, so John flew home, got his ride, and drove out. To his parents' chagrin, a year out of college Dan had ended up as his brother had before him: He skied during the day and slept in a van at night.

The Egan brothers happened to be skiing at Tahoe's Squaw Valley in the winter of 1988 when a friend mentioned that the North Face clothing company was holding tryouts for its new Extreme Skiing Team. Dan and John decided to give it a try. The audition process was straightforward, if dangerous. The skiers would hike up to the top of a steep slope or the start of a couloir (a steep, narrow chute in a rock face) and then show what they could do. Both brothers successfully navigated the impossibly steep terrain and made the team, which consisted of six skiers. The North Face Extreme Skiers would travel the globe, following the winter, hitting dozens of high-altitude ski slopes and resorts. And the whole thing would be captured in a series of movies. For Dan Egan, it was the beginning of a life-long love affair with skiing and film.

Walking in Warren Miller's Snowshoes

It's hard to remember now that in the late 1980s, there was no such thing as "extreme sports." Skateboarding, BMX biking, and surfing had been around since the 1960s, of course, and active leisure pursuits like mountain biking and bungee jumping were gaining in popularity. But for the most part, these sports remained on the fringes of the national consciousness. One activity in particular, snowboarding, was gaining traction (or trying to lose it, as the case may be) in the mid-1980s, but it was the exception that proved the rule. Snowboarding had been outlawed at numerous ski resorts across the country, and the ban helped to fuel its "bad-boy" image and only added to its allure for young people. There was one person, however, who seemed to be ahead of the curve when it came to seeing the potential of extreme sports, and skiing and snowboarding in particular. His name is Warren Miller.

Born and raised in Hollywood during the Depression, legend has it that in 1937 Miller traded $2 and a pair of steel roller skates for his first set of Spaulding pine skis. He never looked back. As soon as he got his hands on an 8-mm camera, Miller began making skiing films, and he has been making them ever since—and at a prodigious rate: He has released 500 and counting. With the widespread adoption of the videocassette recorder (VCR) in the 1980s, Miller's films really took off. His earliest successful releases were adrenaline-fueled documentaries that showed seemingly insane young men jumping cliffs on impossibly steep terrain. The movies were immensely popular with skiers, who bought them by the armful at ski shops.

A typical segment of a Miller film might show two skiers jumping out of the doorway of a moving aerial tram, plunging for 20 or 30 feet, then landing in a splash of deep snow, only to regain balance and shoot off down a hill, skiing in fluffy white powder up to their necks. Beautifully photographed and carefully set to music, the films were filled with natural wonders and glamorous risk taking, and they typically included clips showing the lighter side of skiing and ski resorts (his blooper reels are legendary). As for his subjects, they were not actors but simply expert skiers willing to take major risks to gain a few minutes of filmed immortality. Miller was once asked how he got his skiers to put their lives on the line for his films. "Simple," he quipped. "We buy them a lift ticket!"

John Egan was one of the many skilled skiers who benefited from Miller's free lift tickets. By 1988 he had already appeared in several Miller productions. For him, the North Face Extreme Team films were simply more of the same—though with the added benefit of additional screen time. But Dan—who was new to the world of ski films but, unlike his brother, had business classes under his belt—immediately saw more than just a chance to cliff jump on camera.

"I saw an opportunity for sponsorships, sure, but I also developed a marketing plan for the two of us and pitched retail stores and ski shops," he said. "Our marketing line was 'The Egan Brothers: skiing to double your exposure.'" To his dismay, Dan also quickly discovered that John had never even had contracts for his sponsorship deals—going back to 1978! It had all been done on handshakes. He immediately set about reorganizing their deals, creating sponsorship contracts for the two of them, as well as for the other members of the North Face team. "At this time, even though snowboarding was hitting, there was really no platform for extreme sports," he said. "All the money—and it wasn't a lot, we're talking hundreds or a few thousands of dollars—was in sponsorships." Initially, the brothers got free equipment and not much cash. But as extreme sports grew in popularity and visibility, things began to change. Within two years the brothers were bringing in about $75,000 in sponsorship deals; two years later the business was grossing more than a quarter million.

Dan quickly saw the potential in the business of making ski films. Ski competitions were ephemeral, but the VHS business was booming, and videos had a long shelf life. With his skiing, he was doing what he had always wanted to do, but at the same time he was learning about film production, as well as the business side of filmmaking. Soon, Dan began to pitch the North Face Extreme Team films to ski shops, and then he started to appear in and distribute Warren Miller films. He eventually became the company's distributor for the territory east of the Mississippi.

But he still lived to ski. Dan traveled the world, skiing on every continent. "I would go to Europe for a month at a time, then come back for a while, then go off again. I remember we had a free parking space for the van in Denver, so we weren't even paying rent!" Dan was living the life of a rock star (as he terms it), perhaps without the excess cash but with plenty of ski groupies and lots of partying. Still in his early 20s, he was in peak physical condition and loved to travel. He and his friends began taking video equipment wherever they went, and it was an ideal time to be young and carefree and to have the ability to get it all on film. "We were in Berlin when the wall came down," he recalled, "and at that moment it occurred to me that wherever CNN was, that's where we wanted to be. That was the exposure. We were living the extreme life," he continued, "on and off the snow."

Death Comes to Elbrus

The fall of communism in the Soviet Union began to dictate the brothers' travel schedule. For an extreme skier in search of new mountains to conquer, it was a glorious time. High peaks once off-limits to Western visitors were now open to anyone with the time, money, and guts to climb up and ski down them. Thus, in May 1990, Dan and John Egan were among a group of about two dozen skiers from around the globe, including associated journalists and hangers-on, who would attempt to summit and then ski down Mount Elbrus in Russia. While not a technical climb, Elbrus has a history of severe weather and, over the years, many climbing deaths. And these weren't the only obstacles. The climbers in the group spoke seven different languages, and their experience levels ranged widely from expert mountain guides to recreational skiers. Still, at the time Dan had no inkling that it was an ill-fated trip and one that would leave him near death at 18,000 feet. It would also change his outlook on life.

On May 2, after acclimating for three days at a refuge at about 14,000 feet, the group set out, on skis, to climb the few thousand feet to the summit. But, they soon found, they were not the only group attempting to do so. According to a film Dan made during the trip, there were 13 other expeditions trying to summit Elbrus on the same day. During the previous days, the weather had been inconsistent, the sun shining at some times, then turning stormy just a few minutes later. Though a storm had raged the night before, the morning of May 2 dawned sunny, and the guides decided to push ahead through snow two feet deep.

Dan and John decided to split up; Dan would climb with a French journalist, and John would go with Tom Day, their cameraman, at a slightly slower pace. It had begun to snow lightly at about nine o'clock that morning, but by ten o'clock, the snow was falling heavily, and visibility was fading. Dan and his partner pushed past their guides in an attempt to reach the summit and ski down—this, after all, was the point of the climb. At noon, deciding that continuing to the summit was unwise, John and Tom turned back, rescuing several other members of the group who had become disoriented. But because the storm was coming up the mountain from below, Dan, who was slightly higher, had a clear view of the summit, not yet hidden by the snow and cloud. He was determined to press on. Becoming separated from his French climbing partner, he hooked up with Alfred, a Spaniard who was also climbing with their party. At 18,000 feet, breathing became labored. Finally, at 150 feet below the summit, both men decided to leave their packs, reasoning that they could get to the top quicker without the extra weight. It would turn out to be a terrible mistake.

Just 40 feet from the top, the two exhausted men literally ran into Sascha, a Russian guide and a member of another party attempting to summit Elbrus. The guide was searching for two Italian climbers who had become separated from their group. The three men climbed the last few feet to the summit together.

The storm hit the summit with fury, dropping foot after foot of snow on the three climbers. Though the severe weather, they knew, would make climbing down treacherous, the men decided against staying the night on the summit. "We had left our packs, so we had no food, no water, and no supplies," Dan recalled. With each passing hour, he knew, their chances of making it down were dwindling. They needed to make a move, and quickly. They decided to leave the summit and try for base camp at once.

But the trek down, Dan knew, would be more dangerous than the climb up. Large sections of Elbrus were covered by a vast glacier, and the glacier was spider-webbed with crevasses. The deepening snow and poor visibility made these fissures in the ice impossible to see. Skiing down, he knew, was out. They would have to walk. But if the men wandered off course, the risks of falling into a crevasse and being severely injured, or killed, were high. Nevertheless, Dan, Alfred, and Sascha began their descent, wearing crampons and using ice axes to control their speed on the frozen sections of the mountain.

After several hours of arduous descent, they ran into another group of climbers, Russians. With Sascha leading the way and translating, their expanding group moved excruciatingly slowly down the mountainside. Then, with no warning, one climber lost control and began sliding. In seconds, he disappeared into a crevasse. Racing to tie a rope around his chest, Sascha dove into the crevasse after the man. Tying the rope around the injured climber (his face was smashed), Sascha shouted up at the remaining members of the group to pull the injured climber to the surface. Then they lowered the rope a second time and pulled Sascha out.

At that point, Dan realized they could not continue their descent in darkness; it was just too dangerous. Each member of the group began to dig his own snow cave, and Dan wondered if he was digging his own grave into the mountainside. Though they had camping stoves, the Russians—perhaps from lingering suspicion of anything American, notwithstanding the fall of the Berlin Wall the year before—refused to share the water they made with the American climbers.

Soaked and freezing, vomiting blood and hallucinating, Dan feared he would not make it through the night. "I definitely thought I was going to die," he remembered. "I saw the bright light, the angels, the whole thing. I had known people who died on shoots, but I guess, at age 24, you never think it's going to happen to you. You think you'll live forever." Just then, an image appeared at the opening of his cave. It was Sascha. He curled up next to Dan, the Russian guide using his body heat to keep Dan warm. He reassured the American that they would survive the night and make it down the next day.

But the following day, things got worse. During their second day of descent, another climber fell into a crevasse, this time breaking a leg. "I felt trapped," Dan later recalled in a film about the incident. "We could not find our way back to the [snow] caves, and now Sascha was rescuing another climber. This was Russian roulette. Eventually, we're all going to end up in a hole," he said. "I was just trying to prepare myself mentally for my turn."

The Russians wanted to dig additional caves and stay on the mountain another night, while Dan and his group were determined to keep going. The storm might linger or even become more severe, Dan thought, making a later descent even more difficult. Eventually, the group split in two, with Sascha deciding to trek down with Dan rather than wait out the storm with the other Russians. While tending to the injured men, he directed Dan to the group of huddled Russians to borrow additional rope they would need for their descent. Reluctantly, Dan approached the freezing men, men who had been unwilling even to share water (and the fuel needed to make it) with other desperate climbers. "Staring into their eyes," he recalled, "I saw hatred, fear, and the unknown." Nevertheless, he took the rope, and, leaving them shivering in their snow caves, he went back to join Sascha and the injured men.

With Dan and Sascha breaking trail, the small group of weary and injured climbers trekked through four feet of snow for three hours, finally finding the tongue of the glacier. After resting overnight off the glacier, Sascha returned to the mountain to rescue the stranded Russians. Dan and the rest of his group eventually found a road and made it down the mountain. To this day Dan credits his survival of the ordeal to Sascha.

Though suffering from exhaustion and exposure and each thinking the other had perished on the mountain, Dan and John had a joyous reunion at base camp. Dan, Alfred, and several other climbers were transferred to a Paris hospital, suffering from exposure and frostbite. But they were the lucky ones. The storm had taken a heavy toll: Of the more than 50 climbers and skiers who tried to summit Elbrus on May 2, 1990, more than half died in the storm. But while he survived Elbrus to climb and ski again, Dan wondered if perhaps his nine lives might be running out.

Televising the Revolutions

His ill-fated trip to Mount Elbrus changed Dan. He began to be more aware of the risks he was taking and of his own mortality. An article he read in the *Wall Street Journal* led to an interest in "Young Men's Immortality Syndrome," a condition for which he appeared to possess all the symptoms. "The only cures were death, the birth of a child, and a near-death experience," he said. He had not experienced the first two, but he had been very close to dying, and he decided to change his life. He stopped drinking, and he concentrated on growing his business. He became a content provider, providing ski footage to Warren Miller and other film companies, all the while retaining the rights to his material. He began to intersperse his extreme skiing footage with documentary material about the places he visited, interviewing indigenous mountain peoples about their culture and way of life. He traveled to Kurdistan during the buildup to the Gulf War; to Moscow's Red Square in 1991, the day Armenia declared its independence from Soviet rule; and to Lebanon in 1993. In March of that year he learned that Paul Ruff, a fellow extreme skier and friend, had died while attempting a 160-foot cliff jump in the backcountry of Kirkwood Mountain Resort, near Lake Tahoe.

Dan decided he needed a break from extreme skiing.

In 1994, just before the Lillehammer Winter Olympics, Dan got engaged to Mihaela Fera, a downhill racer and two-time Olympian from Romania. A member of the Romanian National Ski Team for 10 years, Mihaela had been skiing since she could walk. The couple moved to New Hampshire in 1995, where Dan began work as the head of a local ski association. Meanwhile, he created the Egan Entertainment Network, a production company that creates and distributes action sports programs for the cable and video markets. He also moved into ski travel and instruction, creating a company called "SkiClinics" that teaches advanced skiing techniques at ski resorts around the world. SkiClinics also fulfills Dan's wanderlust, allowing him to lead ski tours to Alaska, the Antarctic, South America, and across the continental United States.

His love affair with skiing, and especially skiing on the edge, led to a lifetime of involvement with the sport on many levels. But like all love affairs, it had its rocky moments. "The sport has provided me with a lot of pleasure, but also a lot of pain," he said. "I got injured, I had many surgeries, and I was almost killed. And I saw my friends killed. But it was something I just had to do, almost as if it were preordained. I find that most people don't really have a vision of themselves, of their work life, of what they want to be and where they want to be. I knew that I always wanted to be involved in skiing."

In many ways, Dan and his brother John were just a little too far ahead of the extreme sports curve to profit from its financial windfall, at least to the immense extent that today's extreme athletes—with their tremendous exposure from cable television, video games, and the Internet—are able to. The Egan brothers' contracts ranged from a few hundred dollars to about $10,000. But money wasn't the point back then, and it still isn't. "We never made millions," Dan said. "But we didn't care about money. What we were doing was paving the way, and today these guys have found a way to leverage what we created. We took an intangible thing and made it huge."

Thinking for a moment, he continued. "You know, athletically, it's a whole other world now. We were skiing *in* the snow. With the new ski designs, they ski on top of it, and they ski much faster." Today's skis are shorter and wider, and they have tips at both ends, making them more maneuverable. "I remember I was talking to this guy I knew, his name was Jason

Levinthal, way back when; I think he was just out of high school," Dan recounted. "And he showed me this odd-looking pair of skis with twin tips and a short pair of skis with rounded ends called 'ski blades,' and I just didn't get it. And then he said to me, 'Dan, someday kids are going to be skiing backward off cliffs on skis like this.' Well, Jason went on to become a pioneer in ski design and then founded the Line Ski Company. And he turned out to be exactly right."

Today, extreme sports are mainstream. Freestyle skiing became an Olympic sport in 1992, followed by snowboarding in 1998. Even skateboarding is on the Olympic radar. In 2004, numerous skateboarding equipment manufacturers—historically fiercely independent—banded together to create the International Skateboarding Federation, which is now lobbying the International Olympic Committee for inclusion in the 2008 Summer Games in Beijing. Will they succeed? It's too early to tell, but rumor has it that the world's largest skate park is under construction in China. Can Olympic bungee jumping be far behind?

In Dan's mind, the most important thing was always doing what he loved, which was being involved in skiing. "You know," he said, "we were never U.S. Ski Team guys. We weren't world-class skiers. We were just guys who loved to ski. But when I was at Babson, someone once said to me, 'Dan, there is a business there somewhere; you just need to find it.'

And I never forgot those words," he said finally. "And I did find it."

5

SLOP GAGS
AND FROZEN PIPES

The Circus Comes to Town

ESCAPE ARTIST: KAREN DESANTO
GREAT ESCAPE: GETTING OUT
OF THAT LITTLE CAR

Who hasn't pondered at some point—perhaps during a particularly horrific day at the office—what running off and joining the circus might be like? I'm not talking about dreaming of becoming a big-top trapeze artist; many of these are expert gymnasts who spent their childhoods being groomed for competition or at the very least for the Cirque du Soleil. I'm speaking of becoming a circus clown, about big shoes and shaving cream and tiny cars and miserable salaries. For most of us it's a fleeting thought, something considered, tossed around, and just as quickly forgotten. But what about the people who actually do it? How does one decide to become a clown and then sign up for Ringling Bros.? What is circus life really like, and what's happening to the art of clowning? How, as a circus clown, do you raise a family? And do you have to bake your own pies?

Circus clowning has never been an easy life, and clowns, like their jokes, don't always age well. The schedule is tough, the living conditions are less than ideal, and the performers don't always speak the same language. So why do it? Because you love writing gags, you love to entertain, and you're passionate about clowning. Circus life is quite possibly the embodiment of a nontraditional career (at least outside of circus management), but, like many jobs, it too is being touched by shifting economics and competition for the almighty American entertainment dollar. Small circuses are closing, Ringling Bros. is changing, and the cost of tickets is rising rapidly. In particular, clowns are losing their independence—their ability to write and act out what *they* think is funny. It's an art form being transformed (and not necessarily for the better) by the "suits." But nevertheless, if you like the road and you can't picture yourself shuffling papers for the rest of your life, joining the circus is a pretty good escape.

Just don't tell your parents.

There's No Business . . .

There's an old joke about circus life that goes something like this:

A prosperous man takes his son to the Big Top. After every animal act, a stooped, grizzled old guy comes into the ring from backstage with a wheelbarrow and a shovel. The man and his son watch as the old geezer proceeds to carefully shovel up the huge piles of dung and dump them into the wheelbarrow. After the circus ends and the ring has emptied of performers, the two watch as the old guy again comes out and shovels up the piles of droppings and soiled sawdust. His curiosity getting the better of him, the prosperous man brings his son down to the edge of the ring and calls the old guy over.

"Excuse me, sir?" says the man.

"Yes?" the old man replies. "Can I help you?"

"How long have you been doing this?" asks the man, gesturing to the shovel and the piles of crap.

Thinking for a minute, the old guy replies, "35 years."

Incredulous, the man says, "My God, 35 years! Don't you ever get tired of it? Didn't you ever want to do something else with your life?"

"What," the old man says with a sly grin, "and leave show business!"

I thought of this old chestnut as I wandered among the trailers backstage at the Big Apple Circus with Karen DeSanto, one of the circus's three clowns. It was a frigid December afternoon at Lincoln Center—the temperature was in the teens—and Karen was explaining that all the water lines to the performers' trailers had frozen and burst the night before. The pavement was alternately coated with slick sheets of ice and crunchy with salt and filthy frozen slush mixed with wet hay. Most of the performers not only used their trailers for sleeping and changing but also for showering and cooking, both of which were proving impossible without water. Stepping over the hose lines snaking between the trailers, Karen took me to her "dressing room"—basically a table with some makeup containers set up in a permanent concrete pillbox in Damrosch Park, where the circus tent was located. As we walked in, I noticed one of the trapeze artists sitting on the cold concrete floor, stretching her legs.

"Oh good," Karen exclaimed. "We have heat!" Then she looked around, casually surveying the weight-lifting bench, the worn pieces of carpeting on the floor, the piles of costumes and the makeup cases strewn about, and the cinderblock walls with slit windows high up near the ceiling. "Show business!" she exclaimed. "Ain't it grand?"

No Peanuts, No Peanuts Here

There's something depressing, yet at the same time vaguely amusing, about a circus with no peanuts. There are no peanuts at the Big Apple Circus; too many kids are highly allergic. (Where were all these kids when I was growing up, scarfing down bag after bag of peanuts at Ringling Bros.? Were kids simply inhaling peanut dust and dropping dead in their seats, and I just didn't notice? Do they now feed the elephants little airplane bags of Eagle pretzel snacks?)

Also, there are no balloons at the circus either: Latex allergies have taken care of that. No one has yet discovered a child whose illness can be traced (at least directly) to cotton candy, so it's still available. You can also still find your $3 hot dogs, your $2 candy bars, and your $5 popcorn—so salty that your tongue swells on contact and you immediately find yourself gladly shelling out $2.50 for a bottle of "filtered" water. Visiting the Big Apple Circus in Manhattan is not exactly like an afternoon under the Big Top in, say, Topeka. My first clue that this would be a different experience was the woman sitting in front of me, with a towheaded child who appeared to be her grandson. The woman was sheathed in a full-length mink coat, and she was wearing a diamond on her finger that might have blinded the trapeze artists had a spotlight hit it properly.

Circus life is difficult and tends not to be very lucrative, and the contrast between the moneyed audience and the conditions backstage couldn't have been plainer. From the looks of the crowd, these people probably spent more on their dog walkers than a circus clown could pull down in a year. Clearly, no one went into the circus for the money. So why *did* one become a circus clown?

Because the laughter and the applause are addictive.

And because, like the old man scooping dung quipped, it's show business.

•   •   •

Karen DeSanto was born in 1964 in Sacramento, where she grew up. (She describes herself as "41 going on 8, which is about 183 in circus years.") The second oldest of four children, she had one brother a year older and a younger brother and sister. Her parents had adopted her and her older brother Gordon as infants, but her mother later discovered she was able to conceive and had two biological children. Karen said her home life was "difficult." Her father ran a gas station, and money was tight. She remembered her parents as fighting constantly, and she described her childhood as at times "terrible and tumultuous, with lots of hitting and yelling, especially between us kids, leading to a very bad divorce," when she was 7. She left home at 15, living with friends while she was in high school. When she was 17, Gordon committed suicide. "It was very bad," she recalled.

"Everyone, especially my dad, felt guilty," she said, "and a lot of blame was passed around. I was very close with my dad, and I even stayed with him for several weeks just to make sure he would be OK." The family drifted even further apart, and she described her current relationship with her mother and brother as "holiday close," meaning that on the major holidays they call each other and catch up; she remains close to her sister. (Her father was diagnosed with congenital heart disease and passed away some years ago.)

"In high school, I was into drama club and band and anything with a big-group dynamic. My friends were super, and I had many 'adoptive' parents who sort of took me in. And that's when I started clowning." Describing herself as someone who was "goofy, with some cheesy magic tricks," Karen began to do clowning on the weekends, typically earning around $50 at birthdays. Initially, it was all about making some extra money, but she soon found that she enjoyed the performing, though she had no idea, at that point, that clowning might be a career. I asked her what her first clown name was, and she related the following story.

How Not to Apply Your Greasepaint

For her first paying clown job, she was invited by a friend to perform at her child's birthday party in Sacramento. The party was on a summer evening outside, in the yard, and she began her act on the porch, under the lights, as the sun was beginning to set. Karen was in full "whiteface," her entire face covered with sticky white greasepaint. (Today she, and most other clowns, wear the more modern "Auguste" paint, which has a flesh-colored base coat and white paint around just the mouth and chin.)

She began performing the limited tricks in her repertoire. "I had something like two tricks, for 35 minutes," she laughed. Her rope trick went over like a lead balloon. Her sponge ball routine went similarly. The kids looked ready to pass out from boredom. Then she felt a gnat land on her face. Because her skin was coated in tacky paint, the bug stuck fast, desperately flapping its wings in a vain attempt to escape. She ignored it. But within minutes, her face was covered with gnats, all of them stuck like flies on flypaper. It was at that moment that the kids at the party let out a collective "*Eeeeewwww!*" and one child yelled out, "Look, it's Gnatty the Clown!" "That's when I learned that you have to *powder* your makeup so it's not sticky," she said. But the name stuck, at least for a while.

Though her first clowning gig was buggy, she persevered, and she soon found an audience. For much of her early and mid-twenties, she ran a business called "Kids and Us Characters" that provided clowning for various family and corporate functions, and she did well enough to hire several contract clowns to work for her. Eventually, she bought out a competitor. At that same time, she worked a "day job" at the California Secretary of State's office, mostly taking care of the filing for lobbyists looking to do business with the state. I asked her why she took an office job when it seemed, to me, that she didn't need one. "It was a pension, and everyone was telling me to do it when you're young, so I did. It was pretty much paperwork. But I was making good money, with good 'bennies' [benefits]." She attended Sacramento State and a community college for a year, but she never finished, which she regrets. Soon, her business was doing well enough for her to change to part-time work at the Secretary of State's office. She decided to buy a small boat with some friends. "Those were great times. I had the house, the boat, the car, the friends, the vacations. We went to Hawaii twice a year and to Mexico," she said. "Ahh," she laughed, "life was good!"

Getting into College

Things changed when her father became sick when Karen was 29. He came to live with her, and she slowed down to take care of him. His condition deteriorated quickly, and he died soon after. It was at about this time that Karen first spotted a newspaper ad for the Ringling Bros. and Barnum & Bailey Clown College. Up until the late 1990s the Feld organization, which owns and runs the Ringling Bros. circus, also ran the circus's Clown College, essentially a proving ground and training facility for clowns. The college had been founded by Irvin Feld in 1968, at a time when professional clowning seemed to be in decline; at that time there were only about a dozen clowns with the circus, most of them elderly. Fearing his circus would soon be without clowns, Feld created Clown College to bring younger clowns into the business. In a typical year, there might be 2,500 clowns who applied for Clown College by going to an open audition (these auditions were held throughout the country) and performing their gags. Generally, fewer than 50 were accepted. The lucky ones would train for eight weeks at Clown College—dubbed by one wag as the "Yale of Yuks"— in Venice, Florida, with all expenses paid by the Felds. In exchange, clowns who graduated were expected to commit to a one-year contract with the circus. By the late 1980s, clown pay had risen to about $185 a week. (Circus performers are not unionized.)

When Karen spotted the classified ad for Clown College try-outs in San Francisco, she figured, "What the hell, it's only a year," and she threw her clowning gear in the car and drove to the coast. The audition was fairly unstructured, though she described feeling "pressure" from the judges, themselves accomplished clowns with the circus. I pictured a row of elderly clowns (Bozo, Bobo, and so on) in full whiteface makeup, sitting side by side at a long scoring table, a few chomping on exploding cigars, others with their size 40 shoes up on the table, one or two with a squirting flower on their lapels, all in bowler hats and taking copious notes with two-foot-long gag pencils. I imagined that an air horn might ring out if the judges had seen enough of a particular act. Karen told me my mental image was not too far off (except for the horn) but also that the atmosphere was "very serious, and daunting."

At the time (and to this day, if you don't count Cirque du Soleil, which is a Canadian company and is not a "traditional" circus), Ringling Bros. was the only game in town in terms of large, three-ring circuses in the United States. While even into the 1990s there were still a few smaller, traveling one-ring circuses (called "mud shows" in the business), most have died out, as Americans spend their entertainment dollars on other things. For a circus clown, Ringling Bros. was the top of the heap. Karen didn't recall doing any particular act at the audition, aside from some of her magic tricks and perhaps a "slop gag," an old clowning standby that always involves shaving cream, soap bubbles, popcorn, or some other messy substance spewed all over the place. To her extreme surprise, she was accepted. ("I guess they liked my looks," she laughed.) In the winter of 1993, she headed down to Florida for college, where she would perfect her act, write new gags, and learn the ins and outs of traveling circus life.

Riding the Circus Train

Circus life for Karen, as for everyone else, was not rich in monetary rewards. A job with Ringling Bros., however, included a steady paycheck, health benefits, and food and lodging. But the real perk was one not found with any other circus: The famous circus train. Because of the sheer size of the Ringling Bros. circus—hundreds of performers and support staff, tens of thousands of cubic feet of equipment, and of course very large animals, including elephants and tigers—the only practical way to get everybody and everything where it needs to be is by rail.

Ringling Bros. owns two trains, and each train is typically at least 50 cars long, or just short of a mile. "The train runs were just so much fun," Karen said. "You had your own room (even if it was tiny), you could relax and read if and when you wanted, or you could watch the country go by, or if you were like me, you could run up and down and talk to people, have a beer with the band. It was just very communal. I really, really enjoyed those times."

Part of the fun of the circus train was the experience of hanging out with different people from all over the world. For example, to get to the "pie car" (the restaurant car), you might have to walk through cars housing the Chinese troupe, or the Bulgarian troupe, and you could chat with them along the way (assuming some spoke English, which was not always the case). Some troupes had cars with self-contained kitchens, so a trek through a series of cars might bring a range of ethnic food odors too. Some days Karen might see a tiger cub running around the train, or watch as the larger animals were taken from their cars, down ramps, for water stops. "You're in the back door of America. People loved the circus train—it was beautiful, it was colorful, people would park their cars along the tracks and wave and honk their horns. It was great."

The circus train is classified as "passenger/freight," so it took precedence over freight trains running on the same tracks, but it had to idle on sidings while Amtrak trains passed. Thus, trips could be long and slow. Like Amtrak, though, even the circus train had two distinct classes. Greg, Karen's boyfriend at the time (who later became her husband), was also a clown, except that he was considered a "producing clown," which meant that he received writing credits for creating gags, and he was somewhat higher up in the circus pecking order. One of the perks of this hierarchy was a berth in a private car, separated from the "clown car" (where Karen lived) by the animal cars. Karen was forced to wait until the train made a water stop or other stop before she could get out, walk along the tracks, and see her boyfriend. Alcohol was not provided by the circus—the train had no "bar car"—but there was never a shortage: Most performers brought their own booze on board, or they headed to the local liquor mart when the train pulled into town.

One year with Ringling Bros. turned into two, and then three. Karen found she really enjoyed the performing, as well as the opportunity of seeing the country by train. Of course, a clown has to be "happy" (or at least put on a happy face) all the time, and there were days when this wasn't easy. "I always said, 'When you're feeling bad, just go in and talk to the audience,'" Karen said. "They are my energy when I'm feeling tired; they want to hug you and kiss you, and you're making their day, and they make my day too because they feed me when I'm feeling low." The magic of the circus, she added, is that every show is about the same things, about making the audience laugh, or be in wonder, or be amazed. And if you weren't doing that and enjoying it, then you were in the wrong line of work.

Learning to Play an Instrument

Soon, she and Greg began working together to produce gags. A typical gag might be five to seven minutes long, and they would usually come up with the "blow-off" (the end) first and then work backward. "Nothing's new in clowning, that's the thing," she said. "It's all been done before. But the creative process was really fun, and we wrote everything down, and then we pulled various things out and combined them." For example, Karen remembered seeing a clown playing an anvil like a musical instrument, and she decided that it was funny. But that was the blow-off, and they needed a setup. So for the Big Apple Circus, the gag was that she and Greg would play horns (he had a clarinet, she had a French horn hidden under her coat) while being shooed by the ringmaster to "not play here." So they would move to the left a few feet and begin playing again. This went on for a few minutes, and the circus band got into the act as well. At the end of the bit, Karen and Greg unveiled a 150-pound anvil on a stand, which they then proceeded to play using a small tacking hammer in each hand. And they were pretty good. Or at least they seemed to be better than other anvil players I've heard recently.

For Karen, things began to change at Ringling Bros. in the mid-1990s. For several years, she and Greg had been invited to teach clowning at Clown College during the winter months, when the circus was off. But in 1995, the Feld organization began to restructure its shows (which also include "Disney On Ice" and "Siegfried & Roy"). Up to that point, Karen said, clowning in the circus was "pretty organic," with clowns able to create and bring their own routines into the ring. But not long after she joined the circus, she said, things started to change. Word on the grapevine was that the clowns would have less of a say in the gags they did, the costumes they would wear, even the makeup they put on. Management was changing hands, and all of a sudden an insurance guy was telling the clowns what was and wasn't funny. "And at that point, I was too far into it," Karen recalled. "I was over 30, and I thought, 'I can do my thing; just let me do it.' The structure of the show was just changing. Or changing too much for me."

The Ringling Bros. and Barnum & Bailey circus may be "The Greatest Show On Earth," but it's also—if not by nature then by necessity—a business. For Feld Entertainment, there were tens of millions of dollars at stake in keeping the show profitable, and if that meant more structure and less clowning around, so be it. For Karen, Ringling Bros. may still have been fun, but it also began to feel a little too corporate. It was a bit too much like, well, a real job.

She and Greg were married in 1995, and Karen began to think seriously about doing something else, something besides the circus, perhaps moving east to do stand-up comedy or musical theater. Before she could decide, though, Greg was offered a coveted job with the Big Apple Circus, the most prestigious one-ring circus in the United States. He had become well known in clowning circles for producing clever slop gags for Ringling, and after an audition for the owners and nearly a year of wrangling (the owners had initially wanted only Greg, not Karen, but they finally relented), the couple packed up their trailer and moved to New York.

But changes continued apace at Ringling. By 1998, the Felds had apparently determined that there were enough future Ringling Bros. clowns in the pipeline, and a decision was made to shutter Clown College for good. That was the press release reason, at least. Karen believed the decision was driven more by economics, since running the college was costing the Felds a small fortune, perhaps as much as a million dollars a year (and that's just for the shaving cream!). But though the college was closed, it wouldn't be long before Karen and Greg were again asked to teach their craft.

But first, they had to have a baby.

* * *

Karen became pregnant in 1997, unintentionally though not unexpectedly. She continued clowning during her pregnancy, her newfound girth occasionally spurring some odd moments. At one "spot date" (a few days of pickup clowning work at a small traveling circus), one woman pointed to her belly and laughed, remarking that "wasn't it funny" that the clown was "pretending to be pregnant." Karen recalled thinking, "What are you, crazy? What could possibly be funny about a pregnant clown?"

Clowning for (and with) Kids

Karen and Greg's daughter Emily was born in 1998, and I asked Karen if it affected her outlook, if perhaps it changed her view of the importance of money or the necessity of making a permanent home someplace. "In the beginning, after she was born," Karen said, "I remember Greg's parents' saying, 'Well, now that you've got the baby, you guys are going to have to settle down. You can't be doing this anymore.' And the moving around was hard," she admitted. "But we just did it, because the alternative would be to get a 'real job,' an office job, and I'm just not built that way. It would be awful." She considered this for a moment and then added, "Well, I guess you never say 'never,' and if I had to do it, I would: I would sit in an office and maybe do something that had to do with performing." Then she stopped and added, "Ugh, let's not talk about that!" The notion of a *slightly* more settled life, however, didn't seem all that unappealing, provided they could continue clowning in some fashion. When Emily was about eight weeks old, in the summer of 1998, Karen and Greg got their chance. They were invited to come to Circus World Museum, in Baraboo, Wisconsin, to teach clowning.

About 45 minutes north of Madison, the town of Baraboo is the birthplace and original winter quarters of Ringling Bros. circus—the brothers were born in Wisconsin—and it was the town where performers and their animals lived and trained between tours. Circus World Museum is a nonprofit organization that is also a National Historic Landmark. It houses archival material and artifacts detailing the history of circus in the United States, and in the summers it has a one-ring circus show for visitors. The director of the circus asked Karen and Greg if they'd be willing to spend a summer clowning. They agreed that it sounded like fun, packed up their trailer, and drove to Wisconsin.

It was in Baraboo that things began to be a bit more domesticated. One summer soon turned to five summers, and they began splitting their time between clowning and summering in Baraboo and teaching clowning for Ringling (on a contract basis, no longer at Clown College) in Florida during the winters. "It was a really great time," Karen said. "Theatrically, we could do what we wanted, we had a great bunch of friends who were like family, and it began to feel like home." Emily was enrolled in school, and they began to seriously consider the possibility of making the town their permanent base, to the extent that they bought a house near Baraboo—the first for either of them. In 2002, after five years of summer work, Karen and Greg were asked to join the museum's full-time staff, as codirectors of education. With the lure of a good salary, health insurance, and a 401(k) plan, they accepted the offer and started their new life in Wisconsin.

For three years, they visited schools to talk about clowning, circus history, and circus life, and they taught kids how to do circus art. Summers, they would clown for the circus show. "To us, it was the best of both worlds," Karen said. "In the summers, we would do clowning in the big top, and in the winters we would do the education stuff and put on special events, and it was just great for us. We fell in love with the little town, and the whole community just loves the circus, and the shops and businesses are all pretty much built around circus." If there was a heaven on Earth just for clowns, Baraboo was pretty much it. For the first time in 20 years, both Karen and Greg had a place they could call home—or at least a home that wasn't a trailer or a hotel room.

And then, of course, the circus came calling again. In early 2005, their friend Steve Smith, who had been the director of

Clown College, was asked to direct a new show for the Big Apple Circus. They had known Steve for years, and he had served as best man at their Boston wedding—a wedding that had taken place on a Monday, traditionally the circus day off. ("You get great deals on flowers and DJs when you get married on a Monday!" Karen laughed.) Though they were comfortable and happy in Baraboo, they both loved to perform, and the Big Apple Circus, in addition to being a great circus, was close to Greg's family. They signed on for a year, took a leave of absence from Circus World Museum, rented out their house, and packed up the trailer for the drive east.

Clowning Just Off Broadway

The Big Apple Circus, while primarily based in Manhattan's Lincoln Center, is also a traveling show, and it hits, among other places, Atlanta, Georgia; Boston, Massachusetts; Hanover, New Hampshire; Bridgewater, New Jersey; and a few of the outer New York boroughs. The work is typically five or six days per week with two and occasionally three shows per day; each show lasts about two hours. In Manhattan, in particular, the circus is big business: Many shows sell out, while others are closed to the public because all the seats are purchased by corporations and given to employees, schools, or charities (an act known as "buying the tent"). The circus provides on-site schooling both for the children of performers—like Emily—and the performers themselves, a great number of whom are under 17. While most of the performers live in trailers that have kitchenettes, there is a "cookhouse" for the service and support staff who keep the show going. (And these people are fanatical about their work. I was sternly warned not to track sawdust on the recently swept red carpet.) While no circus—with the possible exception of the Cirque du Soleil—is quite like Ringling Bros., many performers, like Karen, prefer a smaller ring and a more intimate venue, one that offers more opportunity for creativity and interaction with the audience. For example, before, during, and after the shows, she and Greg wander through the audience and clown for patrons (and talk to them, and pose for pictures). They also get to write their own material and develop their characters with only limited involvement of management. That's something most performers can only dream about.

• • •

Karen and Greg are not ones to worry too much about money or about the future. They seem content that things will work themselves out and that they will either remain with Big Apple or head back to Baraboo and continue clowning there. But Karen in particular does worry about the future of traditional circus in the United States. Smaller circuses, the "mud shows," are disappearing, leaving only the largest and most expensive shows, where two hours of entertainment for a family of four may cost $200. Cirque du Soleil, part of the *cirque nouveau* movement, eschews animals, and tickets can be $50 or more. The traditional canvas tents, the "big tops," are also disappearing. Cirque du Soleil recently decided to forgo the tent in favor of installing its traveling shows in arenas, and it has five permanent arena shows (including the adults-only skin show "Zumanity") in Las Vegas. And though Ringling left its own tent behind in the 1950s in favor of arenas, 2006 will be the first time in the circus's storied history that its show does not include a ring. (*Circus* is the Latin word for "ring.") But in some form or another, the shows will go on, and the Ringling organization, at least, is hardly struggling. Annual revenues for Feld Entertainment, Inc., are estimated at half a billion dollars. And, of course, circus, as Kenneth Feld recently opined, "has always been whatever the people who ran the circus decided it to be."

Elderly Clowns: Nothing to Laugh At

For Karen, the circus is about the performing, as it always has been. Whether that means clowning for Big Apple or clowning in Baraboo—or both—she hopes to keep going for as long as it's fun. Or at least until her daughter becomes a teenager and is so embarrassed by her parents' profession that's she forced to quit. Or perhaps, she added, until she's too old and decrepit to go on. She's even considered the possibility of moving to Europe and clowning there, where there are dozens of circuses and her craft is highly respected. "In Europe, an old clown is revered," she said, and her face lit up. "Clowns there are like royalty!" she laughed. "I think the European people value the art of physical comedy; they appreciate it so much more. Here, kids are scared by clowns; a clown is a buffoon."

"You know," Karen said finally, perhaps thinking about where she might end up in the future, "in America, an old clown is like a joke." She paused for a second and then continued.

"And not a *good* joke."

$$\textbf{6}$$

HOW TO KEEP A DRUG KINGPIN FROM GETTING TOO RICH

ESCAPE ARTIST: AGENT STEVE SMITH
GREAT ESCAPE: FROM PUSHING PAPER
TO CHASING PUSHERS

What kid grows up badly wanting a career busting drug dealers?

Not many of us, I would offer. That's not to say there aren't the idealistic among us who want to make a difference and see law enforcement as the best way to do it. But I would guess the majority of agents in the antidrug trade have more nuanced feelings about their jobs. They like the action and the excitement, but they don't like the paperwork. Some may truly believe that the drug trade is a dangerous plague on society, but they also know (though perhaps won't admit) that drugs are an unstoppable tide that forever flows to meet demand. And you're never going to eradicate demand. Even the most ardent antidrug crusaders must have a difficult time reconciling the facts on the ground, that more than 40 years of battling illegal drugs has not stopped (or even slowed) their use.

So who becomes passionate about arresting dealers, and why? Lots of people find their passion for law enforcement indirectly. It's a fairly common pattern: They try lots of different things only to discover what they *don't* like: offices and desks, incompetent bosses, jobs that demand long hours for bum paychecks, and career paths that will bring more money but the same level of frustration. There's no rule that says escape artists must single-mindedly pursue their dream jobs from the outset—or that they even know what those dream jobs might be. Finding a career you love is often a process that melds the best aspects of your favorite pursuits while cutting out the stuff you hate. Of course, no job is perfect, and we can't always control whom we answer to (would that it were so). But the story of Agent Steve Smith is helpful in understanding the process many of us will experience before we finally find careers we are passionate about.

Author's note: To protect the identities of the agent and his family members, some names, places, and dates in this chapter have been changed.

Tall Men in an Elevator

To the tall man with the buzz cut in the elevator, the ride down seemed to last for days. Each passing floor dragging by, each person who got in seemed a phantom moving in slow motion.

A nod to this person, a half smile to that person. Tourists. People staying in the hotel. Maybe visitors from Utah or Iowa or some other distant place, taking the family to the big city. See the sites. Maybe take in a show. The tubby husband with the sunburned wife, the restless kids. Civilians. That's what they were. Noncombatants. Ordinary people blissfully unaware of what was going on around them. Who they were riding down the elevator with. Who they were standing next to. Their slow-motion conversations, their meaningless discussions like little flies buzzing in and out of his consciousness. Maybe they give a glance at the box he's carrying. Maybe they wonder for a second what's in there. Maybe the four big men in the elevator with their straight backs and knit shirts and hard stares are delivering sandwiches. Or they're sales reps carrying a box of samples. And the twitchy guy between them? Maybe he was a potential client. But not the boss. Definitely not in charge. The guy glancing around. Nervous. Like he was expecting something. Then looking at one of the big guys when he put his hand on the twitchy guy's elbow. Like a sign, a gesture telling him to calm down. To cool it. No, thought the tall man, these people, these visitors, they were looking, but not really wondering. The tall man was just tired, his mind wandering, trying to concentrate but not able to, jacked up on coffee and adrenaline and 48 hours with no sleep. No one knew who they were or what the hell they were doing there. Because that was the thing about this work. It was almost surreal. The tall man almost couldn't believe he was doing this. Getting paid to do this. And then suddenly the elevator door opened, and everything snapped into focus in an instant. The tourists got out. And then the big men and the twitchy guy walked through the hotel lobby and out into the day, the tall man looking left and right and left again. Checking. Making sure everybody was still oblivious. Still civilians. Still blissfully unaware that the box he was carrying held 10 kilograms of uncut heroin.

Damn, thought the tall man. It was just so much fun. He *loved* this job.

A Mischievous Kid

Like many young people, as a kid Steve Smith had little idea of what he wanted to do when he grew up. As a child, and later as a teenager, he was extremely active, though he tended to favor individual and "extreme" activities over organized and team sports "I played a number of different sports in school, but I was never really good at any of them!" he said, with more humor than regret. He often had trouble "focusing on the task at hand" and described himself as not being particularly motivated; had he been born in the late 1980s instead of the late 1960s, he almost surely would have been diagnosed with attention deficit disorder (accurately or not). Steve and his older brother grew up in a large Midwestern city, and both their parents were professionals. He described his parents as a bit too permissive, perhaps to the point of giving him too long a leash. Though it seemed like a good thing at the time—most of us can remember, as teens, envying the friends whose parents let them run free—Steve admitted that "looking back on it, I felt as though I was drifting, and I'm not sure that was the best thing for me, that maybe I needed a little more guidance."

One result of this somewhat loosely supervised childhood was a tendency to get into minor scrapes and mischief. One day he might show up at home with a black eye, which he blamed on a biking mishap. Another day he might find himself in the dean's office, being pointedly informed that he was lucky he wasn't in Catholic school, where he might deservedly be subjected to corporal punishment. "And that was it," he recalled. "That was the end of the conversation." His grades were mediocre, good enough to get by but not exemplary by any means. In fact, his private schooling may have played an outsized role in reinforcing his tendency to drift along, with the permissive (some might say coddling) atmosphere not uncommon to small, expensive prep schools, where almost no one ever flunked or dropped out. Steve also liked the adventures to be found in the city. He might occasionally sneak out in the middle of the night to go drinking beer with friends in a train tunnel or climb to the top of a bridge or abandoned building. One time, when he was 16, his father had to drive to a neighboring state to bail him and a few friends out of jail on a misdemeanor charge, later dropped.

But though he didn't *know* what he wanted to do with his life, like lots of kids, he had some ideas. "When I was really young, I remember talking to people on the school bus about being in the military," Steve recalled. He remembered an uncle (though not a man he was close to) who was in the Air Force and a grandfather who had worked "for the government," though Steve didn't recall in what capacity. "I remember I was intrigued by it," he said simply, "but I never thought I could really do that—you know what I mean? I wasn't motivated; I didn't know what the qualifications were." Knowing the huge sum his parents must have spent on his education, I asked Steve if he thought his parents would have supported his entering the military straight out of high school. He paused for a minute before answering. "They would have let me if I really wanted to. My parents let me do whatever I wanted to, but they tried to guide me and tell me what the right thing to do was—or what they thought the best idea was. But if I told them what I wanted to do was something else, they'd go along with it. They definitely mentioned college a few times, but there was never too much overt pressure to go." He noted, again, that he wished he'd had a bit more direction, even while he'd had a sense that everything would work itself out somehow. Steve felt that he didn't "assert himself academically" the way he could have, and as a result his performance suffered. "I think it's because I didn't believe in myself as a student, and I didn't think I had it in me, even if I did try."

Hearing all this, it sounded to me like Steve was the Army's proverbial supercandidate, someone who kept a military recruiter up at night, a dream walk-in. He was fit (by high school Steve was well over six feet and lifted weights regularly) and active, with a keen desire for adventure, a middling GPA, and a deep uncertainty about his academic prowess. Thus, I was surprised to learn that he decided to head out west and attend college. He chose a large school, one with a reputation for excellent weather and not especially rigorous academics. Again, he found himself drifting. He described his academic performance as "terrible, terrible." He waited two years to declare a major, then switched to a different one soon after. He did lots of hanging out, drank beer and partied with like-minded kids, and wondered, once again, what he might become when he finished school.

One day during his sophomore year, he went with a friend to the cafeteria; the friend had a loose lunch date with a girl, and he wanted Steve to see her. The young woman, whose name was Jen, showed up, but begged off the date, saying she had a meeting to go to. "I really tried to coax her to stay, to have lunch with us," Steve remembered, "because I thought she was gorgeous, unique looking. And I began running into her at the cafeteria, and one time I butted in front of her in line, and she never let me forget it. She always said, 'You didn't care about me; you just wanted to get your food!'" They began to run into each other on campus, and soon they began dating. When Jen moved to the Southeast for graduate school, Steve transferred to follow her. But he still had little idea of what he wanted to do after he graduated, even as he changed majors for a third time, this time to psychology. "It always bothered me. Again I felt I was drifting, I didn't know what I wanted to do."

Drifting into the Marine Corps

Steve graduated, but he soon found that he would need an advanced degree to practice clinical psychology, something he hadn't really considered before. He had trouble finding a job, partly because he still wasn't sure what he wanted to do. But then one night, while at a party with some friends, he began chatting with a guy who had a splint on his leg. The man told Steve he had just finished the Army's Officer Candidate School (OCS).

Again, Steve found he was intrigued by the possibility of life in the military—and since he now had a degree, he could enter as an officer, not as enlisted. "It sounded to me like a good way to get my career, or at least my résumé, on track," Steve said. I asked him what his parents thought about his potential decision. He replied that he wasn't too worried about what they thought. When pressed, he said they were supportive but troubled, particularly and predictably about the fact that he could be killed. (This was after Iraq's invasion of Kuwait and Operation Desert Storm but a few years before 9/11.) "I wasn't too concerned [about getting killed]," Steve said. "I just knew that something had to happen. Life was too boring, mundane, and I wasn't happy with the way things were going. I wasn't happy with my résumé. I guess I realized that just having that degree would make me like everybody else. The military could give me this adventure and another great thing for my résumé. So I figured I'd do it."

After researching the various branches of the armed services, Steve finally enlisted in the Marines, assuming (rightly) that the training would be the most difficult and the eventual missions the most challenging. Further, he decided he wanted to be in Marine infantry, a group commonly referred to in military circles as "bullet stoppers." Later, he was shocked to encounter fellow enlistees who had somewhat different visions of what life in the military would be like. "I remember we were sitting around the squad bay one night, and everybody I was talking to was saying things like, 'No way am I going into infantry! You'll just be doing this [that is, running] all day long!' These guys were talking about going into administration or working in the motor pool or 'managing assets' or doing some other desk job," he recalled. "And I guess that was fine for a résumé, but I was just flabbergasted. I couldn't believe that people would join the Marine Corps to push papers or work on cars, that they didn't want to be in infantry!"

Of course, in the armed forces you don't always get a choice when it comes to your military occupational specialty (MOS); typically your assignment is based on your peer evaluations and your ranking within your class. Fortunately, Steve got his wish, and after OCS, basic school, and the Infantry Officers Course at Quantico, Virginia, he was given the rank of second lieutenant and an infantry platoon.

•   •   •

Camp Pendleton, just off the coast of California between Los Angeles and San Diego, is a vast, rugged, and mostly dry landscape between the Cleveland National Forest and the Pacific Ocean (and it's the largest patch of undeveloped coastline in Southern California). Pendleton is home to 60,000 military and civilian personnel, and it is the headquarters of the Marine Expeditionary Force and the 1st Marine Division, among many other units. It is here that tens of thousands of marines get their first taste of life in the infantry: Running. Running everywhere, at any hour, running until you can't breathe, until you dry heave on the side of a dirt track, or until you pass out in the desert heat. And then you run some more. Steve arrived at Pendleton late in 1994, and he was given a mixed platoon of about 30 men, a section of fast attack vehicles and a section of man-portable antitank rockets. He moved his men through training that included navigating through forests in the pitch black for days on end, live-fire maneuvers (including shooting live rounds at—and hopefully hitting—pop-up targets), and "The War," a multiweek, full-company battlefield simulation.

Again, however, Steve was not satisfied with his performance. "I knew I wasn't doing well, and I think it was purely due to lack of studying, again." Further, after three years with Jen, he had said goodbye to her when he joined the Marines, knowing that his travel would make maintaining a relationship impossible. I asked him how he felt about the possibility that he might have to kill someone or perhaps carry out the military policies of an administration whose general views he might disagree with. "Of course I thought about [killing], but my general feeling was that it would be them or me. They tell you only to follow lawful commands, and up to that point, I hadn't been dismayed with anything the U.S. government had done. So I didn't think they'd send me to do something stupid," he said, and laughed. "If Congress says so, then I'm there! But the thing that gets me," he continued, "is people who sign up for the military, or the reserves, and then they get a [combat] assignment, and they say, 'No, this is crazy,' or they start mouthing off against the government. And it's like, listen, you signed up for a position that takes your voice away in that respect. Because the whole machine stops if people start asking questions [about orders.]"

Float and Fat Bodies

After 18 months of "work-up" (training) with his men, in late 1995 Steve and his marines went on "float." Though the name perhaps implies an ocean voyage to a distant trouble spot in need of American intervention, the reality of the float for Steve was more prosaic, and immensely more boring. For Steve's platoon, it consisted of a six-month deployment sitting on a ship bobbing off the coast of East Africa and, well, floating. The year 1995 was one of relative geopolitical stability, after Somalia and before Serbia and Kosovo. Instead of keeping order, defending the defenseless, or invading a country possibly harboring WMD, Steve's marines found themselves on a destroyer playing video games and watching movies.

"It was 54 days straight of being on the water," Steve recalled. "It was so boring, it was like being on a football team and never, ever getting to play." A relatively small problem that took up a majority of Steve's time were his "fat bodies," marines who were out of shape and didn't want to get in shape; it didn't help matters that there was nowhere for them to train, or run. "My main problem was with my sergeants. It's difficult to keep them busy, and when they're not busy, that's when they start screwing around." Steve began to feel trapped in his uniform, worried that he had signed on for a lifetime of waiting around for something, anything to happen. He and his men longed to fire their weapons, to attack an enemy position, to do something with their training. Instead, they played cards.

To make matters worse, Steve's evaluations were poor. At one point during the work-up to float, his commander told him, flat out, that he didn't understand why Steve's men listened to him, because Steve was, essentially, a bad officer and a poor leader. Steve recalled that he was perplexed by this harsh criticism. "My guys listened to me, they respected me," Steve insisted. "They were good guys, and they did what I told them to do. And my commander was still saying, 'I don't understand why they listen to you, but they do.'" I asked if perhaps his superior offered some advice, or some help. Steve said the man was dismissive. "He said, 'Do what you have to do, and if it works, I'm not going to get in the way.' Basically he was just a jerk." Steve also missed Jen terribly—and in 1996 the use of e-mail in the military was not widespread—so with little to report, he settled for composing mundane letters and the occasional depressing phone call.

Eventually Steve's ship steamed to the Middle East. Again, he saw no action, and his stories of stir-crazy soldiers getting into trouble reminded me of scenes from the film *Jarhead*, with marines in full battle dress, armed to the teeth, looking for any excuse to shoot off their weapons. Finally, after six months of boredom, he had had enough. He had signed on for excitement, and instead he had spent his time waiting for something to happen. "Every marine I was with wanted to do something. And one of the reasons that pushed me to get out was that I felt as if I was never going to do anything. And I couldn't stand wearing the uniform and not *doing anything*!" After float, he returned home and was frocked (scheduled for promotion) to captain, his commanding officer's negative performance reviews apparently notwithstanding. Upon his return to Pendleton, he called Jen and asked her to marry him. She agreed but with the understanding that she would not be a military wife. Steve's four-year commitment was up, and he couldn't imagine another four years like the ones he had spent. He decided to get out.

Steve and Jen were married in the fall of 1999, almost exactly two years before the attacks of 9/11.

Watching the Towers Fall

Like many former soldiers, Steve was unsure about a career choice. He thought he might like a career in law enforcement, perhaps with the FBI, DEA, or CIA. "I wanted to be in a dynamic job, doing something interesting, I didn't want to be stuck behind a desk," he said. But, again, he lacked confidence in his abilities. "I didn't think I was qualified, I didn't have a lot of confidence that I could be hired to do that. So I kind of fished around for whatever was available." He discovered that finding a career that suited him was a challenge. Never a man happy being sedentary, he dreaded putting on a suit and sitting in a cubicle. But he was willing to try. Partly as a result of an informational interview with a friend of the family, he decided on finance. He landed a job in financial sales with a large investment banking house. "I was intrigued by the idea of managing people's money, and I knew the sales aspect would be a challenge for me, so I decided to give it a try," Steve recalled. "I liked the fact that that I would be interacting with people and that I was going to be selling them on an idea, because you can't tell them what [an investment] is going to do. You can tell them what it has done, what it's proposed to do, and what you hope it will do. But you have to sell them on the idea. And it was a challenge. But I didn't do so well." Steve said that part of the job included facing one of his biggest fears: Getting in front of people and presenting ideas—as he put it, "getting in people's faces." I pointed out, of course, that he had done exactly that in the Marine Corps. "Yeah," he laughed, "but they don't have a choice!" In the real world, he noted, and especially in the financial world, when the shit hit the fan, his clients could walk away.

In the late summer of 2001, still living and working on the West Coast, he was assigned to a training session in a high-rise building in West New York, New Jersey, just across the Hudson River from Manhattan. On the morning of September 11th, the group of trainees was having coffee and just getting settled when a man burst into the conference room through a side door and announced that a plane had just hit the World Trade Center and that "it must be a terrorist attack." The instructor tried to keep a lid on the chaos as Steve and the others in the room ran to the large windows, trying to get an understanding of what was happening. Soon, the group moved as one to the cafeteria, where huge windows afforded a clear view of the towers. They watched as flames poured out of the upper floors of the South Tower, the black smoke drifting in greasy gray plumes across the city. "Then," Steve remembered, "the second plane hit. We watched it, and it looked like a massive explosion, with all the debris flying out of the building. And I watched, and I saw [the North Tower] come down. And that's when all hell broke loose." People ran for the exits, or they got on the phone to call loved ones. As in many high-rise buildings on that day, people were evacuated, unsure if a coordinated attack on skyscrapers was in the offing.

In the weeks that followed, as it became clear that the nation was gearing up for a colossal retaliatory strike against the Taliban in Afghanistan, Steve was certain he would be called to serve. However, because his status was "inactive ready reserve," when he left active duty he was not assigned to any unit. "I thought everyone was going to get called up," Steve said. "And I was ready to go."

Back to Business

Had he been with a unit, Steve almost certainly would have been called to serve in Afghanistan (as well as in Iraq, a few years later). But, as it turned out, the invasion was quick and successful (or at least seemed to be so at the time), and Steve was not recalled. Instead, he and Jen decided to move to the East Coast, to be closer to her family, and Steve requested and was granted a transfer to another division within his company, this time working in commercial lending.

Again, though, he was unhappy. "My boss was terrible at making decisions, and that was a huge difference from the Marine Corps. People made decisions to the best of their judgment at the time, and they'd make them and not hesitate," Steve said. "This guy was taking his sweet-ass time for every little decision. And it was driving me nuts." Another problem was that Steve was "naïve" about how business was done "behind the scenes," about how corners were cut. "It was my first real [exposure] to seeing how things get done in business, and it's really just about driving numbers," he recalled. Nothing the company was doing was illegal (to his knowledge), or immoral (he believed), but Steve's boss wanted him to make problems go away without telling him how he did it. Because his boss didn't want to know. "Lots of times, I think he just didn't want to make decisions because he knew they could get him in trouble," Steve said. Again, the contrast with the military was striking. "Big business is not about service; it's about making money, however they can make money," Steve added, "and if that means doing better service, then hey, they're going to do better service. But until someone comes along and tells them to do that, they're going to beg, borrow, and steal!"

Steve said that, because he was trying to do too much too well—perfectly and accurately analyzing portfolios ("doing the job the way it should be done, not how they wanted me to do it")—his performance reviews were not very good. In addition, he was working extremely long hours for very little money, and he had a two-hour commute each way. The couple also now had a young son, whom Steve saw only rarely. He would come home late at night, and Jen would see that he was absolutely spent. "I was just so frustrated and overworked, and they just kept piling work on me because they weren't really expecting me to do the work they'd given me." He found himself in the unenviable position of trying to do good work for a boss who didn't care. "I was miserable, working outrageous hours and weekends, and the only thing that kept me going was that I knew I was doing my best," he remembered. "But they didn't care."

Finally, things came to a head. Steve and Jen sat down, and Steve told her, flat out, that the job was killing him. "She said to me, 'Listen, you've got to do what you love to do,'" Steve said. Jen asked him what he thought he wanted to do, what would make him happy, what he wanted from life. They talked about his dream jobs, again placing law enforcement at the top of the list. I asked him whether, in addition to the excitement of such a job choice, patriotism played some part in his choice. "It did, that's definitely a part, but it is also the feeling of wanting to give something back," Steve said. "Listen, I'm lucky. I have a lot, and I know I'm lucky. It's just this feeling of doing something for others—it makes you feel good."

A few days later, Jen handed Steve the application for the Drug Enforcement Administration and told him to fill it out.

Secrets and Lies

Though it took more than a year—a year that included polygraphs, background checks, and interviews by government officials with his high school friends and neighbors—Steve was accepted as an agent-in-training. As in the Marines, he faced several months of rigorous boot-camp-style exercises, as well as classroom work. He finally worked up the courage to tell his parents what he'd done, and they were supportive, mostly because they sensed he had finally found the career he'd been searching for. Their pride in their son, however, was tempered by the fact that Steve had instructed them that they could not tell their friends what he was doing. It was the beginning of his encounters with the secrecy his new job demanded.

"The thing is, with this job, you might have someone who you know and trust, but you never know who *they* know, who they talk to, and I remember my boss said to me, 'You are going to be putting guys in prison, and some of them are going to get out someday.' I prefer to keep [what I do] a secret, and maybe it's some sort of selfish thing, where it makes me feel more important than I am," he laughed, "but also, listen, if my name gets out there, I become a target for . . . whomever. I don't know who my enemies are, and it makes me, and not just me but my wife and my children, vulnerable," Steve said, his voice rising. "And when my wife said to me, 'No one really cares [what you do],' well, that's true among her friends, who are a bunch of suburban women. But their nanny's husband may, or the nanny's husband's cousin may—you know what I mean? And I don't want to cross that path. I don't want to deal with that because when I do have to deal with it, it's going to be too damn late."

Based on the political and national security climate since 9/11, I had assumed the majority of Steve's work would be terrorism related. But, in fact, most of his days (and, regularly, nights) are spent tracking down, shadowing, arresting, and attempting to "flip" cocaine and heroin traffickers connected to the Colombian drug cartels. Which is not to say, of course, that drug running and its attendant money laundering and cash smuggling are not connected to shadowy groups the government believes may be tied to Islamic radicals around the globe. (In fact, the Bush administration is paying close attention to the so-called South American Triangle, a wild, lawless region where Argentina, Brazil, and Paraguay meet and where drug runners reportedly rub elbows with Hamas, Hezbollah and, increasingly, Al Qaeda.) But, for now, Steve concentrates on using wire-taps and cell-phone-tracking software to connect the varied strands of the drug-smuggling web that spans the country. "I love going into the crappy neighborhoods and following people around. I love that there are people out there doing stuff, and very slowly, we creep into their lives, until we're following them, and then we put cuffs on them. I think that it's cool," he said, "that somebody thinks they can get away with something. But, sooner or later, we're going to show up."

Drugs, Terror, and "Painting the Apartment"

The connections between drugs and terror, Steve said, are unavoidable. "In Colombia, you have the right-wing paramilitaries like the AUC, and you have the FARC, the leftists. Those two groups basically run all the bombings and assassinations—

the terrorist activity in Colombia. And in terms of the drug dealing, they are the middlemen, or they are conducting it. And then you have Afghanistan, where you have individuals and groups and tribes running things."

In terms of his investigations, Steve said, the idea is always "the bigger the better." But the reality is that "you get a lead, and you want to pursue it. And most of what we get are phone numbers," he added. "We'll get a name, or we'll get a number, and we'll start taking a closer look at this person. And we'll find some stuff that looks suspicious, and then we'll see who they're talking to, and who those people are talking to, and you get a smattering of people at different levels." One problem with this method is that the targets typically talk in code. "If you've never listened to a dirty conversation, it just sounds like they make no sense whatsoever," Steve said laughing. "It's like two two-year-olds talking to each other, but they're having totally separate conversations, and you're thinking, 'What the hell are they talking about?' But once you've been listening for a while, you start to understand." A typical drug-related conversation might go something like this:

Suspect 1: Hey, did you get the shoes?

Suspect 2: Yeah, I got the shoes, but I gotta paint the apartment, and nobody wants the keys.

Suspect 1: But did you show the apartment?

Suspect 2: Yeah, we showed the apartment.

Suspect 1: But what about the shoes? Did you get the shoes?

Suspect 2:	Yeah, we got the shoes. But I gotta paint the apartments. We got four apartments, and nobody wants to rent the apartments.
Suspect 1:	OK, give me the shoes.

To make matters more confusing, most of the conversations are in Spanish, which Steve barely speaks. "But I can hear their tone, and listening to the voices, you can find out who's higher in rank, who's the boss," he noted. "And you don't get that from the transcripts, and the translations make no sense. So you have to go back and listen to the tapes, and you can hear their inflections," he added. "Plus they drop [get rid of] their phones like every 10 minutes and get a new phone. That's one thing I don't understand after doing this job," Steve laughed. "Who the hell buys a prepaid phone that's not dealing drugs or doing something illegal—you know what I'm saying?"

Though he has had to pull his gun, Steve noted that real life in the DEA is appreciably less "amped up" than what we see on television. But, he added, "There are situations that dictate when you have to be assertive and take control, because it's a very dynamic situation, and it's very dangerous to everyone. To me, yeah, it's a thrill, but it's so much shorter [than the process of finding and tailing suspects]. You just roar up in a car, throw someone down, and put the cuffs on them, and then it's over, and it's cleanup time, and you have to process evidence and write reports."

While he's thrilled to be out of a cubicle (except when he's writing reports), Steve said that Jen is having a hard time adjusting to his hours, which include night shifts on the street and in the wire room and the occasional 2 a.m. call that has him scrambling into his car to track down a suspect. "I really don't mind the hours, but I'm bothered that she minds them. But it's really not that crazy. I can go months where I don't go out at night, and then I'll have two or three nights in a row late," Steve said.

I asked Steve how he felt about the long-term effects of what he was doing, taking criminals off the streets. Did he feel it was making a real difference? Wasn't each arrest just a drop in a huge bucket that was constantly being refilled? "There's no question about it; it's a growth industry," he said finally. "There's just no question in my mind that I'm not doing anything other than making sure that a few people don't get too rich in South America."

"But," he added at last, "it's still a hell of a lot of fun."

7

REBELS, HEADHUNTERS, PIGLETS, AND OTHER ADVENTURES DOWNRIVER

Escape Artist: Bridget Crocker
Great Escape: Into the Rapids

Some people find their escapes after years of searching. For others, however, their passions seem, in one form or another, to be with them always—or at least as far back as they can remember. The trick for these people isn't necessarily figuring out what they want to do with their lives. The challenge is turning that passion into an escape, a fulfilling career, and it's often a matter of the right set of circumstances or the right person to influence a decision.

Bridget Crocker came of age in a complex, challenging family dynamic, but one never far from nature. She grew up at the banks of the river that would, when she got a little older, give her the means and the opportunity to travel the world, primarily in a raft. With few friends and no television, her natural escape was the river—a wild, dangerous, yet alluring current that would come to define her life as an adult. As a profession, river guiding is a physically demanding pursuit where lack of skill or training gets people killed. And, still, it is mostly the province of men. Guides are typically passionate not only about the globe's rivers but also about ecology and the environment and the many ways humans are upsetting Earth's natural balance. In this, Bridget is no exception: She has managed to combine her love of the outdoors with river guiding and journalism, fashioning an escape into the few wild regions the planet has left. It's a story of rivers and rapids. And piglets.

Rice and Rapids

The Cagayan River in Luzon, in the northern Philippines, is the country's longest and widest river. Sometimes called the "Rio Grande de Cagayan," the river originates in the countless mountain streams and steep terrain of the Sierra Madre in Nueva Vizcaya Province, then traverses three more provinces—Quirino, Isabela, and Cagayan—as it heads toward the China Sea.

The river passes through the country's "rice bowl," a fertile valley that produces much of the Philippines' rice crop (along with tobacco and corn) year-round. The Cagayan also wends its way through the last remnants of the country's old growth forests, and it supports a number of endemic and endangered species, including the *lurung* fish, the Philippine eagle, and the bleeding heart pigeon. The Cagayan is also a river runner's paradise. The terrain features dramatic changes in elevation, and sections of the river shoot through towering gorges, hitting steep rock walls and making sudden 90-degree turns and drops. Many sections of the Cagayan feature Class 4 rapids, where white water is particularly dangerous and unpredictable, even for experts.

The trip to the Cagayan had been a long time coming. Bridget Crocker and her husband Greg, along with their Filipino partners, were to take a team on a multiday trip down the upper Cagayan. It would be an exploratory descent, this remote northern section of the river having never featured a descent by raft. Running the river during the day, the cosmopolitan group—featuring a soap opera actor, a graduate student making a movie, a Michigan ad executive, a schizophrenic (who had signed up for two different trips under two different names and had two distinct personalities), and a writer and photographer from *Outside*—would camp along the remote banks at night, eating salted squid fried in bacon grease over a campfire. The months of planning had been filled with logistical challenges, including figuring out how to get all their equipment to this remote wilderness area, as well as political hurdles, not the least of which was coordination with locals familiar with the rough terrain and the somewhat suspect security situation in the country.

It was upon their arrival in Manila that things started to fall apart. Word quickly came down from the north that a group of Marxist guerrillas had attacked a local police station in Nueva Ecija, a large province at the southern end of the Cagayan. The bold raid had netted the bandits a large cache of automatic weapons. Worse, rumor had it that the guerrillas had been tipped off about the rafters and their trip north, and they were now planning an ambush on the only road heading toward the upper arm of the river. Bridget and Greg could only assume that the rebels planned to kidnap them. Or kill them. Or possibly kidnap them, hold the group for ransom, and then kill them. Regardless, they could not risk the team's safety, so they quickly began discussing alternative rivers to run.

Unfortunately, most of the put-ins in the region were remote, and they needed a river that was both suitable for rafting and at least moderately accessible by Jeep—and preferably that was not overrun with rebels. They finally agreed upon the Chico, a river in the heavily jungled, mountainous Cordillera Central range, in North Luzon province. Bridget was not totally unfamiliar with the area. She knew, for example, that the indigenous people in the remote Kalinga province had been at odds with the country's central government over plans to dam the Chico and that these conflicts had given rise to armed struggle over the years and many people had been killed.

But as she and Greg tried to tackle the challenges of changing rivers at this late date, she recalled something else she had heard about the region. Toward the end of World War II, the Allies had driven the retreating Japanese army deep into the fearsome Cordillera mountains. Many Japanese soldiers had starved. Others were captured and killed—not by the Americans, however, but by the Kalinga themselves. And in particularly gruesome fashion. The word *Kalinga*, Bridget knew, was derived from an Ibanag and Gaddang word.

Loosely translated, it means "headhunters."

A Room with a View

Bridget Crocker grew up in a trailer park. But for a trailer park, it had a pretty great view. The park was in Jackson, Wyoming, on the banks of the Snake River. Unlike much of the local populace, she was not one of the area's many sons and daughters of privilege, the kids whose parents had huge homes, expansive tracts of valuable land—the kids whose sense of entitlement mirrored their peers' on the coasts. Bridget spent most of her early years living in the Evans Trailer Court, in a tiny trailer she shared with her mother and step-father and brother Josh.

Born in 1971 in Oxnard, California, Bridget moved to Camarillo and then to Wyoming when she was seven, a few years after her mother and father divorced and her mother got remarried to Ralph, a mechanic. Back in the 1970s Jackson ("Jackson Hole" is the name the tourists use) was, and in some important ways remains, a place of unspoiled natural beauty and open space, a place some have called the "Serengeti of the States." Located near the rugged, mountainous border of Idaho and Wyoming—the state that is still the least populous in the country—Jackson itself had just 5,000 residents at the time and is still best known for being a town close to wilderness, specifically Yellowstone and Grand Teton National Parks.

Bridget spent much of her childhood playing in the grass among the willows and huge cottonwoods that lined the banks of the Snake. The river itself—frigid, rocky, jade blue, and for months of the year a deafening torrent of mountain runoff—was theoretically off limits. (Her mother, a nurse, had seen firsthand what the dangerous Snake could do to a person who fell in.) "We didn't have TV, so I spent most of my free time playing by the river," she recalled, "fishing, catching frogs and water skippers, and I also had a few secret spots in the forest." Every now and then, though, when her mother was out of sight, she would spot a relatively calm eddy and take a quick dip in the icy river.

The river's enormous volume—in wet springs as much as 40,000 cubic feet per second—was responsible for carving out some of the nation's most dramatic gorges, including Idaho's towering Hell's Canyon, which is, at nearly 8,000 feet, the deepest gorge in North America. During periods of low flow, the Snake River has many sections of Class 3 rapids, but high flows can turn those sections into raging Class 4s. The Snake River valley was also home to a profusion of wildlife including deer, elk, buffalo, and the occasional moose, many of which wandered into Evans Trailer Court at some point.

Winters, she and her brother Josh would sled down the snow-covered hills surrounding their trailer, first carefully building high "snow berms" to prevent them from flying off the bank and into the Snake. Summers, when Bridget was a teenager, the family would backpack and camp for days at a time, and they would spend one trip a year rafting. She credits much of her adventurous spirit and her love of the outdoors to her mother, who had grown up in Downey, California ("hard-core East LA" was Bridget's description), but had always wanted to get far away. "It had been my mother's dream her whole life to live in the Tetons," Bridget said. "My uncle once told me that when my mom was a little girl, she had pictures of the Tetons and

Yellowstone plastered on her walls!" (Her mom's now an environmentalist and activist, having moved some time ago to remote Montana after Jackson "sold out.")

Things became complicated, however, when Bridget turned 14 and her mother suddenly announced to the family that she was leaving Ralph for Howie, a local environmentalist whom she had met. "I remember we were getting ready for church one morning, and she just said this out of nowhere, and I was devastated," Bridget recalled. "It was just too heartbreaking for me to stay with a family that had changed so much." She decided to leave Jackson and move back to Ventura, to live with her biological father, Mike, a man she barely knew at the time. "This was the beginning of my running," she said. Living with her father did not work out, and when she was 17, she ran again, this time heading back to Jackson and her mother, brother, and new step-father. Eventually, she came to know and like Howie, a man Bridget described using author Steve Chapple's term, "eco-redneck." He taught her about hiking, camping, and surviving in the wilderness—skills she would come to appreciate as she began river running.

She spent her final year of high school at Jackson Hole High School, and she described herself there as "the kind of kid everyone hated": She got straight A's without trying, and she was somewhat withdrawn. She was awkward socially, and she didn't have lots of friends. "It was a very wealthy community, old valley money and tourism money—I remember one kid's family owned the Parker Pen Company," Bridget said. "And we lived in a trailer court." This class divide had been reinforced as early as the third grade, when Bridget recalled being told that she was "trailer trash and would never amount to anything." Again, as she had as a child, she would come home from school and go straight to the river, which was a comforting presence and also an emotional escape. But the Snake was perhaps also a boundary that held her in, an obstacle that needed to be crossed, once and for all. The river was something to be feared, of course, and respected too. But it also represented a way out, a route leading away from Jackson and out into the world.

Getting Outside the Box

An upbringing in and around wilderness typically leads to one of two results: Either the kid wants out at all costs, or she wants more of the same. Bridget found she was drawn to wilderness, but she wanted wilderness that was different. She dreamed of doing something exciting, perhaps writing for *National Geographic*, visiting remote places, and learning about different cultures. After finishing high school, Bridget, like many teenagers, had little fixed idea of what she wanted to do with her life. She knew only what she didn't want. "I didn't like the options," she laughed. "I knew I didn't want to be a doctor or a lawyer, and I didn't want to be in a 'box.'" As her mother had before her, she longed for the unspoiled, to be in places untouched (or at least only lightly touched) by people. The solution presented itself the summer after she finished high school. She began dating Greg Findley, a river guide, who invited her to join him on an 18-day rafting trip down the Colorado River, through the Grand Canyon. With fond memories of her family trips down the Snake, she jumped at the chance. "It was a private trip, just with river guides, and it was just the most magical thing I had ever done, to be living with the river, living with the little tribe, going downstream. And I thought 'This is amazing. This is how I want to live.'" Rafting also compared favorably in her mind to backpacking, Bridget said, because you didn't have to carry all your stuff. "This was like luxury!" she said.

After the trip, she enrolled in a guide school with the purpose of learning how to lead white-water trips and then being hired on by the company after the session. The company, Mad River Boat Trips, was based in Jackson, and it taught its guides on the Snake; it was the same company she had been rafting with as a child. Her backpacking experience had given her some basic wilderness survival skills, though others in her class had similar backgrounds and skill sets. What was unusual was that she was a woman. Of the 25 people in her class, only 3 students were women. (Only 2, including Bridget, were eventually hired.) Though she began guiding more than 16 years ago, Bridget said the number of women river guides is still relatively low; I asked her why she thought this was. She pondered the question for a minute before responding. "I think we have an idea in our society that women aren't as strong as men physically, and I think rafting is something that's perceived as physically demanding—and therefore should be reserved for people who are physically strong," she said. But, she added, perceptions are often changed in unusual ways, and she noticed more women river guides after 1994, the year Meryl Streep starred in the film *The River Wild*.

"That movie changed my life!" she said, only half kidding. "It did so much to raise people's consciousness, and people's attitudes really shifted after it came out." Bridget recalled that the spring before the *The River Wild* was released, she was guiding on the Colorado, and a man came up to her and asked if "she was going to row that big boat all by herself"—a comment that she unfortunately got all the time. "But then after the movie came out that summer, I remember a man got off the bus and said, 'You probably taught Meryl Streep everything she knows, huh?' And it just shifted, just like that, because people now had this cultural reference point for women doing physically demanding sports."

Somewhat surprisingly, Bridget herself does not appear physically imposing. Though at 5-feet-10-inches she's tall, she's a slim 135 pounds and by no means bulky. She said she does consider herself physically strong (as one must be to battle Class 5 rapids on a regular basis), but she credited her success as a river guide more to her understanding of water and river dynamics than to brute strength. "I'm very intuitive about the water, because I didn't have the luxury of the bigger, beefier guys who just muscle their way through to get where they need to be," she said. "I never learned to boat that way because it didn't work for me. I learned how to let the water do the work for me."

From Trailer to Truck

Few people go into river guiding for the money, and Bridget was no exception. Her life and lifestyle were the summer version of a ski bum's. She worked 16-hour days during rafting months (typically late spring through early fall), slept in a tent or in the back of her truck, and in the winters she traveled to the southern hemisphere to follow the sun. In a good summer, she'd make enough to support her winter travels, but she rarely pulled in more than $8,000 a season. (Since you're in a remote river canyon all the time, however, there's virtually no place to spend your money.) "You don't save anything, you don't get rich, but you're able to get your needs met," Bridget said. "You're homeless, but it's more glamorous than that!"

Glam or not, Bridget did begin to see the world, albeit on a shoestring budget. She ran Class 4 white water on the Savegre River in Costa Rica, on that river's first commercial raft descent. She ran the Pacuare, Reventezon, and Naranjo Rivers, also in Costa Rica. She ran the Bio-Bío in Chile, and she became the first American woman to run the Tambopata in Peru. (While on the river, Bridget and her team were shot at by cocaine farmers cultivating land that had once belonged to the Maoist guerrilla organization "Shining Path.") Closer to home, she was on the first raft descent of the Snake River's Black Rock Gorge in Wyoming, and she descended virtually every raft-navigable river in Idaho, Montana, and California.

Dams and Deadlines

While most of the rivers (or sections of rivers) Bridget rafted in the United States are in federally protected wildlife areas, this was rarely the case in the third-world countries she visited. In their quest to control flooding and increase the standard of living via hydropower generation, many South American and African governments are damming rivers at an alarming pace. Seeing firsthand the deleterious effects on both the rivers themselves and on the indigenous populations who have depended upon them, Bridget began keeping a journal to record what she experienced. She had always loved to write, and she quickly realized there was a thriving mini-industry of magazines, travel books, and catalogs in search of good nature reporting from far-off locales. The outdoor clothing company Patagonia picked up her first professional piece, a story about kayaking the upper Zambezi River in Zambia, publishing the story in their catalog. She had been to the Zambezi before, in the early 1990s, but initially only to conduct canoe trips on the river's calmer lower portion. Her boyfriend, Greg, guided raft trips on the hairy upper section, which featured Class 5 rapids and water flows of 100,000 cubic feet per second. Eventually, with more years of major rapids under her belt, she rowed a boat down the upper section, known as the "Boiling Pot."

Other countries, rivers, and stories followed. She and Greg married in 1996, and they decided to start their own river guiding business, which they called "Mukuni," to honor the residents of a Zambian village and its chief, who had become their friends. They led small groups—sometimes wealthy "weekend warriors," sometimes experienced paddlers—down many of the planet's wildest and most remote rivers, from Bolivia to the Philippines to Peru and Costa Rica. They would go to basically any river they deemed even possibly navigable and reachable via four-wheel drive at the put-in location. She and her clients faced a wide variety of perils during these wilderness excursions. While the Kalinga, the Chico River's headhunters in the northern Philippines, turned out to have mostly abandoned the ritual some time ago, injury and sickness (often heat exhaustion and heat stroke) were common experiences. Jungle insects were a constant presence, and venomous snakes often seemed as numerous as the vines on the trees. And the rivers themselves, which of course held countless drowning risks in white-water areas, were crowded with hippos, crocodiles, and any manner of dangerous species.

Including dead piglets.

One morning, a few days into their trip down the Chico, near the Philippine town of Tinglayan, Bridget and her raft mates drifted under a swinging rope bridge that spanned the brown water. Looking up, she noticed dozens of men, women, and children, many sporting intricate tribal tattoos and gripping long, swordlike machetes. As they passed under the gathered Kalinga villagers, Bridget turned toward a splash next to her. Someone has tossed something down at them. Reaching for the bobbing object, she pulled it close with a paddle and hauled it, slimy and wet, into the raft. She gazed down, perplexed, at the small pink carcass of a dead piglet. Carefully, she picked it up. Not wanting to look a gift horse in the mouth, she held it up as she smiled her thanks for this unusual offering.

The crowd stared back as one. Nobody smiled. In fact, they look rather displeased—not the look one was hoping to see on the faces of the Kalinga, who still carry a reputation for fierceness unsurpassed in the tribal highlands of Luzon. Just then,

Bridget's Kalinga guides yelled for her to throw the piglet back into the river. The "offering" was not a gift but a test. The guides explained, perhaps unnecessarily, that no sane person would accept (much less eat) a foul, rotting pig. The Kalinga on the bridge above them wanted to see if their "guests" were smart enough to know better, which they translated as survival prowess. To them, the refusal of the piglet is a sign of intelligence; the acceptance of it the opposite.

Immediately, Bridget tossed the slippery carcass back into the muddy water. She closed her eyes, waiting for spears to rain down. Instead, she heard cheers and whistles from above. Apparently, she had passed the test.

Hearing stories like this one, I asked Bridget if she had thought about being killed or had ever feared for what the future might hold.

"I didn't care if I died," she replied. "I thought that it was the greatest way a person could die. I really had no regard for myself in that way." I pressed her for a fuller explanation: Surely there must have been some sense that she was taking risks that might—in the eyes of an objective outsider, at least—be deemed irrational? She admitted that, especially in her early twenties, she was more concerned with getting out and seeing the world than with what might happen when she got there. "I still had a lot of things I needed to sort out, from my upbringing, and this was the perfect way for me to escape," Bridget said. "Nobody could find me in Zambia, no one could find me in Ethiopia; no one knew where I was." I asked her what she thought she had been hiding from or escaping from. She was silent for a moment before answering. "I had a lot of pain growing up," she said. "It was difficult for me, having parents that were divorced, feeling as though I didn't belong anywhere." She paused, then added, "The river provided me with a sense of belonging that was missing."

Committed for the Season

For a while, Bridget and Greg's business did well. Articles describing their trips began to show up in magazines like *Paddler* and *Outside* (magazines Bridget would eventually begin writing for), and their company was favorably described as working closely with indigenous peoples and utilizing local river guides whenever possible. But it wasn't very long before the couple discovered that running a business required that someone be available to answer the phone and set up the trips. (This was before international cell phones made it somewhat easier to run a company from the field.) By their natures, the two rafters abhorred the idea of an office job, but they also understood it was a necessary evil. They agreed to alternate, with one sitting by the phone while the other guided the river trips; they'd switch roles between seasons.

But it wasn't long before the months apart began to take their toll, and the relationship—and then the business—fell apart. They divorced in 2001. ("River guides can commit only for a season," she said, only half joking, although they were together for 13 years.) I asked Bridget if she had ever worried about money. "Greg and I never had any money. We were always putting everything we had into our next trip, having hand-to-mouth adventures," she recalled. "I grew up with very little money in an extraordinarily wealthy town," she said. "It didn't seem to me that the rich kids were particularly happier than I was. What has always made me happy is being outside and feeling connected to nature. The life I've had as a result of pursuing my happiness has made me very rich in experiences and spiritual, emotional, and physical growth." She added, "To me, these benefits far outweigh anything simple material wealth can provide."

Still, even spiritually fulfilled people need to eat, and Bridget continued river guiding and writing. Her trips to Central America resulted in contributions to travel publisher Lonely Planet's guidebook to Costa Rica. She began to work on turning her journal into a collection of travel stories highlighting her decade rafting the world's wildest and most isolated rivers—perhaps something akin to a river runner's memoir. In 2001, she moved to Ventura, California. In an apartment with an expansive deck and a view of the Channel Islands, she began what has become a more settled life. Initially, she focused on her writing and took a job as a writer for Patagonia. She also took up surfing and diving, and she created a Web site, bridgetcrocker.com, to chronicle her adventures.

Today, she leads rafting trips on the Kern River for Whitewater Voyages, a commercial rafting company, but she no longer works a full season. Instead, she's a bit more selective, making the occasional journey to South or Central America to guide a rafting trip, typically in conjunction with a freelance writing job. She continues to surf, and she writes when she's not river guiding or surfing. She also dives and travels regularly to the Channel Islands and is preparing for a first descent down a river in Arunachel Pradesh, India, in 2007. "My focus today is on my connection to the natural world, not on escaping a painful past," Bridget said. "Rivers and my relationship with them have consistently nurtured me and brought me back to myself. They molded me into the woman I am today, one who is strong and adaptable. I am so grateful for the extraordinary life I've lived and the incredible growth and connections I've had from following the water's path."

8

YOU'RE FUNNY, BUT CAN YOU TELL A JOKE?

ESCAPE ARTIST: HENRY CHO
GREAT ESCAPE: FROM HOUSE PAINTING TO HEADLINING

Not long ago I was at a comedy club near my house, and a comedian named John Evans begged the audience to buy his CD, which he assured us was the best CD he had ever burned himself on his home computer, and which came in a jewel case from Target. He explained that he had "tried regular jobs and wasn't good at anything." The only thing he knew how to do well, he said, was tell jokes. It wasn't necessarily a great line (and it surely wasn't original), but it was near the end of his set, the audience was in a good mood and slightly drunk, and it worked.

Later on it struck me that good comedians make enough money that they don't have to do anything besides stand-up to make a living. And they don't want to. They like to tell jokes and will continue to do so, period, even when working is no longer necessary. How else to explain Jerry Seinfeld? The man is worth hundreds of millions, doesn't need to work another day in his life, yet still appears at small comedy clubs and does his sets regularly. As with most performing, comedy is like a drug, and the bigger you get, the more you want your fix. But for every Jerry Seinfeld and Ray Romano (who also continues to do stand-up), there are scores of comedians on the circuit who work because they have to. It's not an easy life, but the rewards are significant if you're successful: Great money for a few hours on stage per week. More than that, making people laugh is *fun*.

Lots of people are funny. Or think they're funny. But who decides to become a professional comedian? Typically it's a career that's best begun early, before you have a family. It's a craft that's as much about *how* you tell jokes as the jokes themselves. It's also about finding your niche in the market. What's your hook? Will you work "blue"? Are you laid-back? Combative? Are you an insult comic? A prop comic?

Whatever their focus, all comedians have one thing in common: the desire to never, ever have a "regular" job.

Welcome to Mississippi

At least the show wasn't a chicken-wire gig.

For a comedian, the chicken wire was always a bad, bad sign. That was when the comedy club owner installed a heavy mesh screen that separated the stage from the patrons. When an owner knew his comedians needed protection from his customers, Henry Cho understood, it was rarely a good omen. And anyway, the "cage" might protect you from the flying plates, bottles, and ashtrays, but it did nothing to stop the backwash and cigarette butts that easily made it through the openings. He always made sure he placed the mike stand well to the back of the stage during these shows, just in case something made it through the wire.

Henry had done more than a few chicken-wire shows, but this gig, at least, wasn't one of them. But it still didn't look good. It was 1989, and this eight-city tour with a bunch of top comedians (Jerry Seinfeld, Tim Allen, Larry Miller) had brought him and Tim to Jackson, Mississippi. But just days before the show, they had gotten word that the club where they had been booked had gone bankrupt and shut down. Rushing to find a room to fill the schedule, the promoter had sent them on a four-night stand to a place neither man had ever heard of, a room called "The Dock." The Dock was not a comedy club but rather a local bar and restaurant set on the edge of the Ross Barnett Reservoir, a popular summertime recreation area. After taking the stage the first night, Henry had shouted to be heard over the din of boat engines starting up, while Tim struggled with the soundboard (there was no sound technician). At one point, Henry looked over at the board, and Tim had his head in his hands. He appeared to be crying. A few members of the audience looked as though they had never even seen a Korean before—much less heard one from Tennessee with a thick southern accent. Other patrons appeared to be one joke away from starting the "Freebird" chant. A few men appeared to be passed out drunk or dead. At least they had taken the Confederate flags down. Right considerate of them, Henry thought.

Now it was the second night, and Henry was determined to make a go of it. He opened with a favorite joke: "Hey, my name's Henry Cho. I'm full blooded Korean. I was born and raised in Knoxville, Tennessee. [Beat.] So I'm South Korean." A few snickers and murmurs and then nothing but the clink of bottles. He began to wonder. Almost afraid to know the answer, he addressed the audience: "How many of you were here last night?"

The response came from somewhere in the darkened back of the room.

"We all were," said a man.

Henry swallowed. He was going to need some new material.

The Only Cho in the Phone Book

No one ever told Henry Cho he should be a comedian. No one ever called him a "cutup" or tagged him as the class clown. He was never sent to the principal's office for making fun of the teacher. He never did little comedy routines for his family or told off-color jokes at the dinner table. In fact, he entered the business on a fluke, via some dumb luck. His parents, both immigrants to the United Stated from Seoul, had two potential career choices for him: doctor or veterinarian. He wanted to play baseball.

"I was born in 1961 in Knoxville, and my father was a scientist at Oak Ridge National Laboratory," Henry said. "My father was the smartest man I have ever known. He had two doctorates and 14 patents. Today, he would have gone to Harvard. Back then, he went to Warren Wilson Junior College in

North Carolina. When I was born in 1961, the Asian population in Knoxville consisted of five people: My parents, my two
older sisters, and me." From kindergarten until his senior year
in high school, the only Asians Henry ever saw were his rela-
tives. "By the time I hit my senior year, I think there were maybe
two Vietnamese kids," immigrants from the war. He did not
recall experiencing any significant racism growing up, though
being an Asian from Knoxville would later play a role in his
act. "I used to tell this joke, about how when I was young the
other kids and I used to play cowboys and Indians. They were
always the cowboys. I was the cook," he laughed. His mother
was a special-education teacher.

He attended the University of Tennessee for six years, off and
on, initially as a premed major, then jumping to engineering and
then to business, specifically to accounting and then marketing
"because that's where all the girls were." In January 1986, on
a break from work painting houses, he spotted an ad for a
Showtime competition called "The Funniest Person in America." The pay cable station was sponsoring blind tryouts in
cities across the country, including Knoxville. He told his two
roommates that he was going to apply. "They said to me, 'But,
you're not even funny,' and I told them, I know, but I have it
figured out," he said. Jerry Seinfeld had come to Knoxville a
few months before; Henry had seen the show, and it made an
impression. Though he didn't have any real material, he was
quick witted and pretty good at thinking on his feet, and he was
at least original: a good ol' baseball-playin'-UT-attending southern boy, with a thick southern accent. Except that he was Asian.
He figured that was enough to at least get him started.

Lucky 13

He applied for the contest (no audition was required) and was picked thirteenth. Unfortunately, the show was only accepting 12 people; he was the first alternate. Then, in a stroke of luck, someone dropped out at the last minute, and he got the call to perform. He worked out some material with his friends, mostly short stories about what it was like growing up as the only Asian in a southern American city. Though he didn't know it at the time, 10 of the other 12 contestants were actually working comedians. After watching the first few contestants take the stage of The Funny Bone in Knoxville, he had a flash of panic. These people were real comedians, with actual jokes and stage presence. He was just an Asian guy with a funny accent. What had he been thinking? He told his friends that he was going to go on stage and try not to embarrass himself, and then they would leave.

He began his 5 minutes with a true story, except that he told it as if he were an Asian with little command of English. Henry recalled the moment: "I talked about how I was in school, and this girl came up to me and began speaking very loudly and very slowly, saying 'Do . . . you . . . want . . . to . . . be . . . in . . . the . . . international . . . section . . . of . . . the . . . student . . . annual?' And then I looked at her and said, 'I reckin' not.'" The audience roared, and he was off. Watching Henry's audition that day was Gerry Kubach, the owner of The Funny Bone chain, which at that time had 18 outlets across the country. After the show, Kubach approached Henry and asked him how long he'd been in comedy. "About 5 minutes," was Henry's reply. Sensing a new talent, Kubach offered Henry a job as an "opener": introducing the visiting comedians before they took the stage at The

Funny Bone (known as "emceeing" in the industry). He'd need about 15 minutes of material. Henry accepted, and he began work that Wednesday night, two days after his first-ever comedy gig. On Friday, he dropped out of college.

When Henry told his parents about his decision, they were stunned. "It just hit the fan," Henry laughed. "My dad freaked. He did not understand what a comedy club was and that there was a club circuit; he only knew from seeing comedians on *The Tonight Show*. I told him I was going to drop out of school and be a comedian, like the ones on Johnny Carson. And he replied, 'Are you on Johnny Carson?' And I said, 'No, not yet!' And I remember my dad said, 'Let me tell you one thing: Don't ever make fun of your mother.' And I never have. But I make fun of my dad!" Henry forbade his parents from seeing his act for more than a year, making them wait until he was comfortable with his material. The first few nights, his heart was pounding, and even 20 years later, he still gets nervous stepping onto the stage in front of a crowd. "It's like Carson once said," Henry noted. "If you don't get a little nervous, something's wrong."

I asked Henry if he felt he was destined to be a comedian. "You know, had I gone up there that night and failed, I probably would not have pursued it. And if that twelfth contestant had not dropped out, I doubt we'd be talking today," he said. "So many of my comedian friends have said to me over the years, 'Henry, you don't know what it's like: The first time you go on stage, you're supposed to eat it. And then you're supposed to wait a week and think it over to see if you can get the courage to go on stage and try it again. You walked on stage on a Monday and immediately became a comedian.'"

Destiny or not, there was still a long and not always fun road ahead.

Comedy Condos on the Circuit

Professional comedians often note that lots of people are funny, and lots of people can write jokes. There are even quite a few people who are funny, can write jokes, and are able to stand in front of an audience and tell them well. None of this, they note, is the hardest part of being a comedian. Being able to handle life on the road is what separates the pros from the pretenders. To make money as a stand-up comic, you have to be on the comedy club circuit—and that means travel. Lots and lots and lots of travel. Ask any working comic and you'll get the same response: The road is the great equalizer, and day after day, night after night, it takes its toll.

After a few months of working at The Funny Bone, Henry was offered the chance to travel to the other clubs in the franchise, which were scattered throughout the country. He began as the emcee, earning a few hundred dollars a week, but he quickly moved up to "feature," the middle act that comes just before the headliner. ("I realized pretty early on that to make money in the business, you had to move up," Henry noted.) As a feature act, he started to earn some real money, typically between $650 and $1,000 per week—with his actual stage time limited to about 30 minutes per night a few nights a week. That was the easy part. But it's not just the ability to write and tell jokes that separates stand-up comics from the rest of us. It's also knowing that you're not going to sleep in your own bed for 300 nights of the year and knowing you're going to be on stage for 280 of those nights, "duking it out with a bunch of drunken people," in Henry's words. "In most of these places, you show up and the only two people you know are these two other comedians," he said, adding, "and you don't even really know them." He continued, "I remember there was one point where I had like 31 shows in 29 days, and the travel was just a killer. It was a series of jets, then puddle jumpers, then rental cars, then driving to some place you had never been. At night."

Though the comedians' housing and travel were paid for by club owners, the accommodations were often a punch line. Many of the comedy clubs owned or rented crappy two-bedroom apartments nearby; this arrangement was cheaper than putting the talent up in hotels. These places, known in the industry as "comedy condos," had often been on the receiving end of late-night, drunken free-for-alls featuring the comedians and anybody they knew or could pick up the night of the show. "I remember I went to this one comedy condo," Henry said, "and the place actually had no front door. The door was just gone." A comedy condo in Cincinnati had two pieces of paper taped to the cabinet: One was the club address and the show times, and the other was a schedule of local Alcoholics Anonymous meetings. Henry used to travel with his own set of sheets and towels rather than use those provided (or, as was often the case, not provided). Occasionally, he would wake up in the morning only to discover the other comic staying at the condo had yet to return from the previous night's partying.

Along with the incessant travel came the loneliness. With full days to fill in strange cities and towns and no one to fill them with, Henry chose to take up golf instead of drinking. He also made a conscious decision to work "clean" and in 20 years has never "cussed" (his word) on stage. Working clean meant that some opportunities were open to him that might have been closed to other, "blue" (profane) comics. One such opportunity was the chance to open for Jerry Seinfeld. In late 1986, Henry had been opening at The Funny Bone for a popular comedian named Bill Engvall. Engvall, also a southerner, had broken into the business at the Dallas Comedy Corner, and he had appeared on *The Tonight Show*. (Engvall now tours with Jeff Foxworthy and the Blue Collar Boys comedy troupe.) In 1987, Henry got a call from the owner of The Punchline Comedy Club in Atlanta. Seinfeld was scheduled to appear, and he was looking for a clean opener. Though *The Seinfeld Chronicles* (later *Seinfeld*) had yet to air, the pre-TV Jerry Seinfeld was still one of the biggest names on the club circuit and a major draw. (And, of course, he has never worked blue.) After their first show together, Seinfeld came up to Henry and paid him a compliment. "I remember he said to me, 'Don't ever stop doing stand-up,'" Henry recalled. "'I know you probably want to do other things, but don't stop doing stand-up because there are very few people who do it well, and you do it well.'" Seinfeld's point was that Henry, like many other comedians, would get seemingly tantalizing offers from Hollywood for various projects—many of which would never materialize—but that, even if he viewed stand-up as a stepping stone to an acting career, Henry should continue with it. For a young comedian, it was an important message. (And, interestingly, one that Seinfeld himself has continued to heed. He continues with stand-up despite his fame and tremendous wealth.)

After their last show at The Punchline, Seinfeld invited Henry to come on the road with him and open at several other clubs, and Henry accepted. After their tour, Seinfeld returned to Los Angeles to begin filming his sitcom, but he told his fellow comedians about Henry, and soon Henry was fielding calls from several other top comics looking for a feature man. But like countless other comedians before him, for Henry the siren song of potential television and film opportunities proved very difficult to resist. "I saw Billy Crystal and Steve Martin doing it, and I figured that starting out in comedy was a great way to eventually do films and television." But the nature of the comedy club business meant that to make money, you needed to be on the road. There were not enough clubs in the Los Angeles area to make a good living, and moving out there meant giving up the circuit while you pursued your acting dreams. You couldn't do both.

Henry decided to stay on the road for one more year, and it was a wise decision. The National Association for Campus Activities offered him a series of 90 college shows in 1988, and it enabled him to save enough money for a move to the West Coast and a break from the circuit. In January 1989, with money in the bank, he packed up his car and drove to Los Angeles.

We'd Like Your Show to Have a Dog

One of the oddest things about the entertainment industry (OK, one of the many, many odd things) is the fact that it's a creative business run by people who are often not very creative. The screenwriter William Goldman famously described Hollywood as the place where "nobody knows anything." The executives who sign up shows that become hits (often through luck, timing, and little else) are lavishly rewarded and credited as creative geniuses. But those who are truly on the creative side of the business (the writers, actors, cinematographers, set designers, and so forth) can see their fortunes made and unmade by the bean counters in corner offices—pulling down seven-figure salaries—who have never written, acted in, produced, or designed anything. For a comedian used to writing and presenting his own material, this lack of creative control can prove maddening.

As Henry began to get into the Hollywood rhythm and "take meetings," he soon found that while he was able to land small guest roles on shows like *Designing Women* and *The New WKRP in Cincinnati,* creating his own show and maintaining some measure of control over it was almost impossible. Not long after he arrived, he met with a network executive to pitch a sitcom in which he would play a young Korean American who returns from a southern college to live with his newly widowed father. He recommended his friend Pat Morita, whom he had known for a few years, for the father role. The executive liked the concept, but he insisted that the show would be funnier if Morita spoke "broken" English. "I said no way," Henry recalled. "You have to understand that at this time, there had never been a show like this, where it was just a regular American family who happened to be Asian—in many ways similar to what the Cosby show was doing for African Americans. But this guy insisted on having broken English. And I just said forget it."

After Henry left the project, Morita followed, and the show was later retitled *All-American Girl* and offered to fellow Korean-American comedian Margaret Cho (no relation to Henry), who accepted. (Henry advised Cho, a longtime colleague, not to do it.) Margaret Cho was directed to lose 40 pounds and to act "more Asian," whatever that meant. *All-American Girl* was canceled after one season, and Margaret Cho later admitted to serious problems with drug and alcohol abuse following the cancellation. "The show was just awful, negative and derogatory," Henry remembered. "It might as well have been [set in] 1960." He added that perhaps even more unfortunate than the show itself was the negative impact it had on the likelihood of another sitcom with an Asian-American star making it on television. (There are still none on the major network and cable channels.) Henry, who grew up in the only Asian family in a very southern city, had encountered more Asian stereotyping in California than he had in Tennessee. "I had to move to Los Angeles to experience racism!" he laughed.

Nevertheless, he continued to find occasional television and film work (*Revenge of the Nerds III, McHale's Navy*) while at the same time pitching his own ideas. (At one pitch meeting, a network executive insisted that Henry add a dog to his potential sitcom because *Frazier* had a dog. He politely declined.) He lived in a two-bedroom apartment in Hermosa Beach, played lots of golf, and took some stand-up gigs to pay the bills. At the same time, his agent pounded the bricks to book him on *The Tonight Show*, the Holy Grail for any working comedian.

Emperor Carson

Johnny Carson was the comedy kingmaker. For decades, comedians argued over the relative merits of the star's peculiar approach to stand-up comics, particularly his tendency to play favorites. If you got the Carson wave and were "called to the couch" after your act, you were golden. Conversely, you could feel like a pariah (and a failure) if you were left standing like a scarecrow as the show went to commercial, Carson clapping politely. But hate him or love him, there was no debating the power Carson wielded and the opportunity that an appearance on his show represented. "Everything goes up once you get on *The Tonight Show*," Henry said. "Your stand-up money goes up, places that you wanted to work but couldn't are open to you, you get to call some shots, everything happens." Though he had already appeared several times, to good reviews, on CBS's short-lived *The Pat Sajak Show*, Henry was desperate for a shot at *Tonight*.

The call finally came in early 1992. Henry was booked to appear on the show, and he began to try out new material on the road to see what worked and what didn't. Then, just weeks later, Carson announced his retirement. Immediately, the show's producers began lining up *The Tonight Show*'s longtime guests to pay their tributes, and young comics who had never appeared on the show fell off the radar. "It was like, 'Who are you going to have on, Henry Cho or Bette Midler? Robin Williams or Henry Cho?'" Henry laughed. "But fortunately when Jay took over, he asked me to be on—I was actually his first comic—and actually he thought that I had been on before, not realizing it had been Pat Sajak's show, or Arsenio Hall.

Everyone just remembered a guy standing behind a curtain and assumed it was *The Tonight Show*."

Henry opened with one of his favorite jokes:

"I live in LA; lot of Asian people here. It kinda freaks me out 'cause back home I was it: I was the only Asian guy within like four states. Made it kinda tough as a little kid though. You guys remember playing army as a kid? You guessed it. I pretty much hated that game. All my buddies would say, 'All right, Henry, it's the neighborhood against . . . YOU!'"

Then he talked about hating the earthquakes in Los Angeles. "I've been through a couple. The first one really scared me to death, but it helped me, 'cause I was bowling." His segment ended to raucous applause. Henry glanced over at Jay. The new late-night king was waving him over. His appearance was officially a huge success. "I *destroyed*. And then it all started again," Henry said. He was invited back just six weeks later. "What happened in 1989 happened again in 1992. The phones were off the hook." He realized his star was rising quickly on the club circuit, and over the next year he did about 20 weeks on the road. But it wasn't long before he realized he was sick of Los Angeles, tired of the endless auditions and pointless meetings and double-talking executives. And he was tired of never being grounded, of never feeling like he was "home."

Tobacco Farming and Friday Night Videos

In early 1994, Henry packed up again, this time moving back east, to Nashville. For $165,000 he bought a 62-acre farm outside the city, which, as long as he was able to bale and sell hay twice a year for $1,500, brought in a decent tax credit. In a fairly comedic twist on agricultural subsidies, the federal government offered to subsidize Henry's hay farm as long as he didn't grow tobacco. "The government said to me, 'We'll pay you money as long as you don't grow tobacco,'" Henry recalled. "And I said, 'Well, I'm not growing it anyway, so why don't you just give me the money!' But I didn't really see how I could take money from the government for not growing something that I wasn't planning to grow. I told them to give it to somebody who *was* growing tobacco but said they wouldn't."

After several additional *Tonight Show* appearances, his road money had gone up considerably, and Henry was now able to make a good living working fewer weeks per year. Then, one day, he got an odd phone call. A well-known late-night producer for NBC named Gary Considine had seen a few of his appearances and was impressed. Would Henry by any chance be interested in a hosting job? *Friday Night Videos* had an opening and was looking for a comedian host. (The show, which debuted in 1983, was once hosted by the well-known comedian Richard Belzer.) There were six weeks left in the season, and Henry agreed to do three weeks provided that he did not have to move back to Los Angeles. The producers agreed to fly him in for the taping, which was on Wednesdays. "By the third week our ratings had tripled, and I signed on for another three weeks, and then another, and another." The hosting gig was a breeze—there was a short monologue at the beginning and then just quick intros and outros between videos—and lucrative, particularly since it was one day a week and it did not preclude Henry from doing stand-up on the weekends. He hosted for two years, and he left shortly before the show was canceled due to the growing adoption of cable and the near-ubiquity of MTV.

Henry was now making a very good living from comedy, with the added benefit of also having the luxury of time to do television and film projects. I asked him about his attitude toward money. "I never really cared much about it," he said. "In Knoxville, growing up, we were comfortable but certainly not affluent by any means. When we had a chance to move across town to a fancier neighborhood, my parents chose not to, because we'd be moving away from all our friends." As an adult, Henry did not spend lavishly. Unlike fellow comedians Seinfeld and Leno, both of whom have what are among the most valuable privately held car collections in the United States, Henry was not an especially conspicuous consumer. Though he had bought a house and the farm, he saved most of his earnings. In 1995, he met his future wife, Amy, at a Christmas party. They were married in Arab, Alabama, in 1998. At this point, Henry needed to work just eight nights a month, headlining, to make a good living. He also became a solid corporate draw, doing private shows for large companies like Bridgestone and Kellogg. Such shows were more lucrative than comedy club gigs, though (following Jerry Seinfeld's sage advice) he still used the club circuit to work out new material. In 2000, his first son, Jackson, was born, followed by Grant in 2002 and Tate in 2005. With a family comes financial responsibility, of course, and Henry's success has enabled his wife to stay home with their children. And his corporate shows, which pay five figures and are an hour long, have given Henry the luxury of being a "stay-at-home" dad most days.

Cable Takes Hold

Though a few large clubs remain, the comedy club boom that lasted from the mid-1980s to the early 1990s has now faded. Many small live venues have been displaced by the huge audiences delivered by various comedy-focused cable outlets and the seemingly endless stream of comedians on DVD (including Henry: Warner Bros. Records released his first DVD/CD in July 2006). Still, the well-known chains—The Funny Bone, The Punchline, Carolines, and the Improv among them—are still active, and they are still virtually the only way to break into the business, at least on the performance side. Not long ago I asked Henry if all stand-up comedians aspire to be a Jerry Seinfeld or a Ray Romano or a Drew Carey. That is, do all comedians have the ultimate goal of becoming a successful sitcom star who no longer needs to work for a living? He chuckled. "That's a lofty goal. It's like saying you want to be an astronaut but you have poor eyesight," he said. "You can count on the fingers of two hands, maybe one hand, the comics who have had successful shows while maintaining creative control," that is, doing the shows they want to do. And naturally the success of sitcoms often depends on external factors out of a comic's control, things like time slots and competition. It seems that for most stand-up comics, what they want to do most is tell good jokes and not have to sleep in the "comedy condos" too many nights of the year.

In some ways, Henry had the good luck of great timing. He started his stand-up career when he was very young, during the club boom years, and he established his credentials on the road while still single, before he had a family back home; being on the club circuit is not exactly conducive to marital bliss. But beyond that, his unusual background was also a creative mother lode that he mined very effectively, following the old saw to "write what you know." I asked Henry if he ever regretted dropping out of college. He said that he never thought too much about it before he had kids, but now he worries it might be "a battle" when they grow up. Then he related a story about a family member. "I have a nephew who's in theater, and he told me he wanted to be a stand-up comic. So I said, 'I'll make a deal with you. If you graduate from college, I'll help you. And if you drop out, I'll make sure you never work.' One day I took him golfing with some of my buddies who are on the pro tour, and we agreed that they made [playing pro golf] look really, really easy. And later when we went to see some comics I knew, I said to my nephew, 'Comedy is just like golf: The pros make it look easy. But it isn't.'"

9

RIDING
YOUR OBSESSION

ESCAPE ARTIST: JACK VIOREL
GREAT ESCAPE: FROM THE SAND INTO THE SURF

What fulfilling career awaits a person so passionate about surfing that every job he's ever taken has been structured around the need to "get wet" every day? And what happens when the demands of a family clash with the call of the surf?

The story of Jack Viorel's escape is, perhaps more than any other story in this book, about the ways a passion can be molded into a fulfilling career—but also about the dangers that come with such an obsession. Children and single people can afford to be uncompromising with their time, but productive, married adults can't. Successful escape artists find ways to bridge the gap between passion and responsibility. But sometimes, our passions take over, and we aren't willing to compromise, and things get, well, problematic. Jack's story isn't a cautionary tale—it ends well—but it is an instructive lesson on managing our passions and keeping our ids in check.

And if it can be said to have a moral, it's this: A surfer and his board are not easily parted.

Maverick's

Even when you're not about to ride them, the waves at Maverick's, a few miles off the Northern California coast, are enough to make your knees wobble, turn your legs to jelly, and make you clutch your surfboard that much tighter.

As a spectator, floating on your board out of the surf zone, you don't worry about actually catching and riding one of the monster 60-foot waves smashing in; you leave that to the pros. Instead, you worry about drifting just a little too close, then getting sucked into the break, a wall of water six stories high coming down on top of you, tossing you like a rag doll, holding you down, holding you under and unable to surface through the "washing machine"—the turbulent white water that's impossible to pierce from below.

You worry about a two-wave hold-down—not just a single massive "rogue" wave but a series of them, one after another, too close in sequence to allow you to come up for air. As a spectator, even one lying prone on a surfboard watching the pros, you imagine what it's like to "tombstone"—to look up from below only to see your board held vertically, sticking out of the water, a sign to the rescuers on jet skis that you need help. *Fast.* You watch in awe as the professional tow-surfers—the ones who get dragged in behind jet skis, the swells simply too gigantic to paddle into while lying on a surfboard—begin the dangerous dance, the ride of their lives and perhaps the one that could end their lives, and you wonder.

You wonder about the courage it takes to ride these massive waves, and you wonder about the kind of person with the guts to do it, and keep doing it, forever. You marvel not just at the sight but at the sound of the ocean—angry and violent, unforgiving, crashing like a loose freight train, like a thousand tons of steel rushing off the tracks and into oblivion. You take in the fury and the beauty and the lone surfer wanting nothing less than the perfect wave, an impossible quest, at once chasing and trying not to be caught by the sea. You hold on tight to that surfboard, and you stay just far enough from the break for safety, just close enough to see and to hear. And then, with your knees still wobbly but the thrill of the action giving you a glow inside, you smile. Because the surfing bug bit you too, long ago, and it's both a curse and a blessing, an anchor and a lifeline, an itch that must be scratched but can never be eliminated.

A magnificent obsession.

The Coldest Winter I Ever Spent . . .

El Granada may be coastal California, but it's a far cry from the forever sunny, perpetual-summer paradise of Beach Boys' harmonies. Just north of Half Moon Bay, about 30 miles south of San Francisco, the area is socked in by drizzle, mist, and fog for much of the year. The ocean water is cold. The cloud cover keeps the air temperature cool, and, like San Francisco, even August days can demand a warm sweater. The poor weather has its benefits though. It has kept this beautiful stretch of forested coastline unspoiled, blessedly free of the suburban and exurban development that has crept, as inexorably as the tide, farther and farther outward from the Bay area over the past decade. For those looking for sun, or at least some semblance of the popular notion of California dreamin', the inland "silicon cities" of Burlingame, Redwood City, and Palo Alto offer better weather, more jobs, and at least a modicum of cultural enrichment.

But for Jack Viorel, El Granada has its own particular set of special pleasures. This misty coastal community—where wood-framed houses are still affordable and you can ride your bike on winding, sand-covered streets to the beach—offers what really matters and what those inland temples to dot-commerce can never deliver: consistent, solid waves, day after day, month after month, year after year. Enough waves to last a lifetime.

If surfing is Jack's magnificent obsession, it didn't start out that way. He didn't even ride a surfboard until he was in college, in the early 1990s. In high school, in Roseville, California, near Sacramento, and later at the University of California, Davis (UC Davis), he played football. That was his dad's obsession, not his. "My dad would be down on the sidelines, yelling, screaming, no matter what was going on, no matter what I did, right or wrong," Jack recalled. A former college football standout himself, Jack's father, like many former athletes, badly wanted to transmit and transfer his competitive nature to his son. In spite of these attempts—or perhaps because of them— Jack was never able to conjure up the brutal, competitive spirit that his father and the game of football demanded. Though he stands a solid 5-foot-10, with a washboard stomach and hugely muscled arms that would seem perfect for tossing cornerbacks and safeties like rag dolls, no one would mistake Jack for a football player today. His easygoing demeanor, laid-back bearing, and soothing, almost gentle voice are more evocative of late-night beach barbecues than pep rallies and smash-mouth 'ball. "I just never had that competitive edge," he admitted. "Football wasn't for me. Though I didn't know it back then, I was a surfer at heart."

Surfers (and surfing magazines) often talk about the "surfing lifestyle"; more pejoratively, its aficionados are sometimes tagged with the moniker "beach bums." But both terms, positive or negative, generally describe a type of carefree, utilitarian, perhaps even subsistence-level existence where money and the accumulation of possessions hold little sway. Surfers are occasionally compared to hippies, although the comparison is less than precise. Though drugs like pot may play a supporting role, the natural environment is considered in many ways sacred. There's always an element of wanderlust, and the surfing lifestyle is rigorous and physically demanding.

Growing up, Jack cared little for money. "My parents both worked really hard. My dad was a private investigator, and he was rarely at home. My mom was a teacher, but she always had two jobs. I guess seeing them, I just never developed the philosophy of money. It just never had any value for me, beyond where it could get me for travel. I always thought anything was possible," he said. "And I always believed you could figure out a way to keep your life unorthodox, to keep all your options open."

Snow to Surf

The obsession actually began with snowboarding. At UC Davis, Jack was less than two hours from the mountains, where he picked up snowboarding during the winters. "I was pretty wild growing up, riding freight trains, doing crazy things with friends, and eventually I was introduced to snowboarding," he remembered. Still relatively new at the time, snowboarding was considered edgy, the province of skateboarders, a controversial "corruption" of skiing that many resorts had banned or relegated to outer regions of their mountains, away from skiers. While snowboarding, Jack began hanging out with a group of guys who surfed as well as 'boarded, and with Davis only 90 minutes from the beach, he began to surf during the spring, summer, and fall. Though not precisely the same, Jack discovered the moves in surfing mimicked those he used in snowboarding to a large degree, and he took to the sport quickly. He soon found himself thinking about surfing all the time: looking at the weather in terms of how it might impact the surf, learning how to read waves, researching equipment, and watching surfing on television.

The surf bug had bitten.

During his senior year, Jack began thinking about a job that might allow him enough free time to surf every day. A friend suggested a seasonal job at a winery: Work the harvest, make decent money, and still have time left to play, his friend suggested. After graduation, Jack accepted an offer from the St. Supéry Winery in Napa. The job was undemanding and unexciting. He worked in the cellars making the wine and earning just $10 per hour. But the money was less important than the hours: He worked just four days per week, and he had the entire winter off. For three years, in the spring, summer, and fall, he worked Monday through Thursday at St. Supéry. On Thursday nights he would drive to the coast, pitch a tent near the beach, and surf for three days, returning to work Monday morning. Winters were reserved for snowboarding in the Sierra, full-time.

It sounded like the perfect life for someone like Jack, an active guy in his twenties without attachments, either personal or financial. I was surprised to learn that, after three years of working in the winery, Jack began to get depressed. Money, especially money for travel, was just too tight. He contemplated going pro as a surfer, but he almost immediately rejected the idea. "You know, for me, surfing is something that I want to keep noncompetitive. I don't want it to be like football." He continued, "When you're a pro surfer, surfing becomes something you *have* to do." He had little desire to add the immense pressure of competition to a sport he enjoyed for its own merits—one of which was a carefree state of relaxation. But even more than that, like many young people, he wanted to do something that made a difference, something with a positive impact on people's lives. "I felt I was not contributing to society," Jack remembered. At the same time, he was adamant that he "didn't want to give up the lifestyle." The question was, what job had it all? What kind of career would pay relatively well, allow him to do something he felt was worthwhile, let him surf every day, provide time for extended vacations in winter and spring for snowboarding, and give him months over the summer to travel—to, as he put it, "experience life"?

The Word of the Day Is "Tube"

The answer, it turned out, was teaching. It was a near-perfect solution. His workday would end at 3 or 4 p.m., leaving two to three uninterrupted hours to surf before sunset. He would have winter and spring breaks, and his summers would be wide open. Best of all, it was a chance to make a positive impact on the lives of young people. He went back to school and received his "multiple-subject" credentials, which allowed him to teach kids from elementary through middle school in any California school where teachers taught multiple classes. He ended up teaching second grade.

For several years, all was bliss. The teaching went well, the kids were great, and his surfing progressed nicely, to the point where he could ride waves up to double overhead (10 to 12 feet) with aplomb. But more to the point, he found that surfing every afternoon made him a better teacher. "[Among the other teachers] I was notorious for leaving right after school. I almost never stayed late for meetings and committees, but ironically I was probably the most popular teacher with parents and students," he explained. "And every teacher I taught with that had their own kids requested me as teacher. I was always the teacher families requested because when I came to school, I was fresh, not bitter." He continued, "I was enthusiastic and energized, not pooped out. I think my approach to life, which has been shaped by surfing, is much like that of a young kid: fascinated by simple things, laughing a lot, playing a lot, excited about everything. I was able to connect with kids because I lived my life much the way they do. And I taught with passion, the same passion I had for surfing."

Teaching also gave Jack lots of time off. He took extended surfing trips, to Bali, to the Andaman Islands in the Indian Ocean, to Nicaragua. Often he would travel (or meet up) with friends, but sometimes he would go alone, with just a surfboard and a pair of swim trunks. Sometimes his trips were risky; friends had warned him that some of his more remote surf locations could be dangerous. As an American, he became a target for harassment. He was often forced to bribe local officials, to "make a donation" to the "new-uniform fund." He quickly learned to hide his cash, to keep only a few dollars in his pockets, enough to buy his way out of trouble.

Occasionally, seemingly carefree adventures took on a much more ominous tone. In Nicaragua, he was robbed—at knifepoint or gunpoint—virtually every day. One day, the true nature of the lawlessness hit him. "I had been sitting in a hut, near the beach, eating a bowl of soup. This guy starts running; he's being chased by a group of men," Jack recalled. The man had been stealing from the local villagers, had been caught, and was being chased through the streets. "They finally caught up with him," he said. "And then they shot him. Right in front of me." He realized that he needed to be more careful, perhaps more discerning with the surf locations he chose.

Lost in the Fog

But the ocean too is unpredictable, and things can go very wrong in the swell as well as on land. One day not long ago, Jack was surfing big waves at Ocean Beach in San Francisco—an area notorious for bad weather, strong currents, and white sharks (often called "man-eaters"). Nearing the end of a long day, a thick fog rolled in. In minutes, Jack was caught in a virtual whiteout, unable to see the shoreline, his surfing buddies, or any lights indicating passing ships or land.

Calling back and forth, the group attempted to stay together using the sounds of their voices. But caught in the fog, Jack became disoriented. Was he paddling toward shore or out to sea? Were the voices he heard in front of him or behind him? As the last of the daylight faded, Jack knew he was in trouble. Alone in 50° water, unsure of his position, and in an area infested with sharks, he tried not to panic. For half an hour, he paddled aimlessly, calling out, trying to locate other surfers. "Hello!" he shouted. "Can anybody hear me?" "Yell if you can hear me!"

But there was nothing but silence, his cries seemingly trapped and enveloped by the fog. Where had they all gone? He had an instant flash of sheer terror. They had all made it back to the beach. He was all alone. He knew full well that a solitary swimmer is much more likely to be attacked by a shark—and that sharks are often drawn to the bright sheen of the underside of a surfboard. But abandoning the board was not an option. He was too tired to swim, and anyway he had no idea where he was, where to swim *to*. Finally, as the sun slipped behind the horizon, he spotted a light off in the middle distance. The fog, though, made it impossible to tell if the light was on land. Perhaps it was a buoy, or a bridge marker?

Regardless, he decided to begin paddling toward the light. The sun had gone down, and it was pitch-black, the fog shrouding him completely. After half an hour of paddling, his arms feeling like lead weights, a building came into focus. The light was from a building! Paddling furiously now, freezing and exhausted, he made it onto the beach and collapsed. Jack looked around to get his bearings. He recognized the area. He had drifted two miles south of where he started.

A Changed Outlook

Surfing had begun as a sport, as a fun yet noncompetitive way to stay in shape. It eventually became a reason to travel, to visit remote places (at least ones with big waves), and meet new people. But soon for Jack—as for most serious surfers—surfing gradually morphed into something much more than a diversion. Surfers talk about how their "sport" tends to expand, how it grows and changes to become not simply about standing on a board in the ocean but something all-encompassing, an activity that carries with it a particular set of beliefs, a daily regimen, and a way of contemplation. On some level, perhaps, surfing leads down a path toward (yes, it sounds clichéd) enlightenment. Though these aspects of surfing are experienced differently, to differing degrees and on many different levels, by different people, Jack leaves little doubt that surfing began to change his life.

"Surfing is about more than concentrating on the next wave," he offered. "It clears your mind, makes you open to new things and new ideas. There's something about the saltwater, I don't know exactly what it is, but it seems to cleanse you spiritually. And without surfing, I would be horrible at the other important things in my life. Surfing gives me the passion, mindset, and positive outlook to be good at the other things I do. The things I get from surfing guide and influence me in my daily life. I think most surfers would say the same." I asked Jack what these things were.

"Surfing has a spiritual element, probably like going to church for some," he replied. "I often feel mentally and emotionally clear and decongested after surfing. Some days are challenging to the point of testing the limits of your courage; other days are playful. I have surfed with dolphins, seals, sea otters, and gray whales. Each day offers up something new, and every surf session seems to have some adventure to it. To really enjoy the surf, or on heavy days just to survive, you have to do so many things that are counterintuitive. You can't fight the ocean; you have to go with it, embrace it, follow its lead, as if you are in a dance with it. Each wave offers opportunities for certain things, but you can take only what it gives you, so you have to be able to read the waves. The best surfers are really in tune with the ocean. I think it is this deeper, more meaningful relationship with the ocean that makes surfing so addicting and such an important part of my life."

I wondered what Jack's peer group was like. Did the people he hung around with have this same philosophy and outlook, this sense that life was not about "work" but about living, about enjoying just being alive? "Most guys I know who surf hold surfing and the ocean in this regard and have thus built their life around a surf lifestyle," he said. "All of the guys I surf with are hilarious characters that are a blast to be around; they are environmentalists, and they care deeply about the ocean. They all look way younger than their years, are fit, and seem to always be happy," he continued. "Those who have kids make great parents, as they seem to have time and a sense of what is really important in this life. They definitely know how to have fun. It's a simple, healthy, relaxed, fun-loving, lighthearted lifestyle, free of the rat race that has devoured many of my college buddies. I really enjoy being part of this small, tight-knit group of guys with the same philosophy of living."

Surfing five days a week can take a toll on a relationship, and up until 1999, it "had ruined pretty much every relationship I'd had," Jack admitted. Girlfriends didn't understand the obsession or didn't care for the time he devoted to it, or they wanted to travel and *not* surf (Ha!). But it didn't really matter. Up until that point, there had never been anyone he'd contemplated marrying or even settling down with. But then, one day, he met Aileen Wu.

Pretty and petite, athletic, with a good sense of humor and a refreshing directness, Aileen had grown up in Atlanta and had graduated from Pomona College. While attending law school at UCLA, she had joined a firm in Palo Alto as a summer associate. One day, she walked into REI, an outdoor store where Jack was working part-time over the summer ("getting good deals on as much snowboard, mountain bike, and other outdoor equipment as I could!" Jack laughed). With the help of a friend, Jack convinced Aileen that they should go on a date— appropriately enough, a "mountain biking date."

Like Jack, Aileen was active and enjoyed the outdoors, especially mountain biking and hiking (though not surfing). "It was a great time to meet Jack," she recalled. "As a summer associate and 'extern,' I still had a decent amount of free time. So Jack and I could enjoy all the outdoor things we both loved to do."

From the start, Jack knew he had met someone special. "As a teacher and dedicated surfer, my relationships never lasted long," he admitted. "Usually the girls would cramp my surfing lifestyle, or they viewed me as a slacker—not motivated or driven to climb the corporate ladder or make any real money." Aileen, he realized, was different. "Aileen was the first woman I had ever met who thought of teaching as a legitimate profession instead of just a low-paying job," Jack said. "She also appreciated instead of resented the fact that I had built a life of leisure as opposed to work and stress. She never made me feel bad about surfing, about doing what I wanted to do. She just accepted it as part of who I am." Soon, Jack and Aileen were dating one another exclusively, and when Aileen finished school, she moved into Jack's house in El Granada.

Damn the Dot-Commers!

Many of the big swells that will eventually reach El Granada begin not in the Pacific but further north, in the Gulf of Alaska. Massive storms take shape in this turbulent region and are often to blame for capsizes and human losses in the extremely dangerous Straits of Alaska. As the dry arctic air whips across the frozen Russian landmass and hits the moist air above the Pacific, it creates a violent collision that generates fierce winds, snowstorms, and towering waves. Depending on the wind direction and speed, the tides, and the size of the swells—information now easily accessible on the Internet—experienced surfers know with relative certainty at night the conditions of the next morning: the direction of the waves, the beaches with the biggest swells and the best breaks, and the areas that will be too choppy to surf.

But El Granada, while a surfer's paradise, is not exactly centrally located, and soon things began to get complicated. "El Granada is on the coast, and my job was in Palo Alto," Aileen said. Though the two towns are just 30 miles apart as the crow flies, the traffic-clogged commute began to take a toll. "During those days, the 101 Freeway was packed with 'dot-commuters' going to their jobs in Silicon Valley," Aileen remembered. "My commute from El Granada brought me straight into that mess, so it could take me as much as an hour and a half to get to work in the morning." Since Jack's school was also slightly north of his house, Aileen figured it made sense for them to leave El Granada and find a place on the peninsula, slightly inland, closer to both their jobs. Jack, however, didn't see it that way.

"Jack saw no reason to move," Aileen recalled. He wanted to stay in El Granada, on the coast, near the best beaches. "He prided himself in not changing his lifestyle to suit his work habit—like most 'working stiffs,'" she said. When, as a compromise, Aileen proposed finding a place halfway between the coast and Palo Alto, Jack wasn't much interested in that either.

Was Jack being selfish about his surfing, about wanting at all costs to maintain his relatively carefree lifestyle, even (or especially) now that there was someone else in the picture, someone with different priorities? In one sense, his obsession was typical of most obsessions: Left unchecked, it grew and expanded until it blotted out everything else, until priorities were reshuffled and lives reordered to accommodate it. But further, there was no getting around the fact that surfing *is*, by definition, a selfish pursuit. It's one person and one surfboard, not a team sport. There was little place for a non-surfer in such a world. In his zeal to surf, was Jack making a mistake by letting his passion get in the way of, well, his *passion*?

Perhaps not unpredictably, for Jack the relative weighting of work versus play lacked a clear and easy solution. The stress of melding his surfing lifestyle with the career needs of another person began to have an impact. In 2000, Jack and Aileen decided to break it off. Aileen moved to Sunnyvale, closer to her job, and Jack, of course, stayed in El Granada. Though they missed one another and kept in touch, neither Jack nor Aileen could see an easy solution: Jack would not leave the coast, and Aileen's job would always be inland, they figured.

Then, a short time later, a funny thing happened. Aileen began to miss the coast. In Sunnyvale, she didn't know any of her neighbors, and she missed her old jogging routes, the miles of beach and the secluded hillside trails. In Sunnyvale, she "couldn't even jog three blocks before coming upon some untraversable highway." In El Granada, they saw their neighbors every day while picking up their mail at the local post office. "Everywhere we'd go, we'd be greeted by name—well, Jack was, anyway," she laughed. "He is such a part of this coastal surfing community; I understand now why he didn't want to leave it. I really enjoyed the rustic character of the place." Though in Sunnyvale her work life was made easier by the short commute, her lifestyle—the time she had for herself—was lacking. And because her free time *was* in such short supply, she began to realize that it was critically important to make the most of the time she did have. It was a notion that Jack had already discovered: A good commute was a poor substitute for a great community.

Back to the Coast

In early 2001, Aileen moved back to El Granada. A few months later, the stock market collapsed and the dot-com bubble burst. As a result, the bloom was off the Silicon Valley rose, and tens of thousands of newly laid off dot-commuters were no longer jamming the freeways. Aileen's commute, though still no picnic, had become manageable at less than an hour. But more than that, when she *wasn't* working, she was happy: happy to be back with Jack and happy to be in a place they both loved. They were married in October of that year, and everything was as it had been. Jack was teaching and surfing, Aileen was working much of the time but enjoying the outdoors when she could, and they knew they would be able to make a life that suited all of their needs. Then, in early 2003 another life- and lifestyle-altering event occurred: Their daughter Gabby was born.

It was an unexpected development. "I had been creative in creating a great surfing life," Jack recalled, "but this was going to be very difficult. I thought adding a kid to the mix might be one thing too many to juggle. I feared having to make a choice, and I hoped I wouldn't have to."

For the first few months, Jack kept his teaching job, and Aileen stayed home. "I could still get a quick surf in after school if I wanted," Jack said, "but I often just rushed home to see Gabby. I would miss her all day long while teaching, so seeing her face after school was an even more fulfilling substitute for surfing, and I appreciated the schedule I had created for myself even more. So many people don't have time for family, and I took total advantage of all the time I had. Every couple of days or so, the surf urge would hit me, kind of like mother ocean tapping my shoulder and saying, 'Don't forget about me,' and I would fit in a surf."

When it was time for Aileen to return to practicing law, they decided they would both continue to work and would hire a nanny. But they quickly developed nanny troubles. One day, a nanny they had sponsored and brought over from Eastern Europe decided she didn't really like the nanny lifestyle. She walked out, leaving a scrawled note indicating she wouldn't be back.

After a few frantic months, Aileen landed a new job that made it financially possible for Jack to stay home if he wanted to, and they agreed it was better for their daughter to have a parent at home, even if it meant some sacrifices. Since Jack's earning potential was significantly lower than Aileen's—and since his flexible hours had meant he was home more anyway—they decided Jack would be Gabby's primary caregiver. But, Jack wondered, how would these new duties square with his surfing? How would Jack, with his now well established surfing regimen, be able to blend child care into the mix?

"For the first year and a half or so of Gabby's life [when he was working], I surfed less than I ever had, just two to three times a week. It was definitely tough surfing so little, especially on the epic days," Jack admitted. "However, I really loved spending time with Gabby, and we were certainly developing a very special relationship." When the time came, Jack said, he jumped at the chance to be a stay-at-home dad. "Gabby and I seemed to have similar personality traits: playful, active, silly, energetic. Gabby loves to go down to the beach and play in the sand; we were taking swim lessons, and we went on bike rides and to the park. I kept telling myself that in time, we would be surfing together every day; I just had to be patient and hang in there."

When Gabby turned two, she began attending preschool part-time, giving Jack more time to surf. Like most hard-core surfers, in the evenings Jack would check the weather and surf forecasts religiously. The next day, starting at about 7:30 a.m., his cell phone would begin ringing with surf reports from his friends. Conditions established, he would schedule to meet up with his buddies at whatever spot had the best surfing on that particular day. He would then make breakfast for the family, drop Gabby off at day care, surf from 9 a.m. to noon, and then pick Gabby up and spend the rest of the day with her. He was even able to continue taking several surfing excursions per year, by himself or with a friend, because of the generous help of his mother: She would come down from Roseville and watch Gabby for a week while Jack traveled to some exotic locale to surf. (In 2003 he went on a combination hiking and surfing trip to Machu Picchu in Peru.) I wondered how Aileen felt, if she was OK with his continued surfing obsession.

"There was a time when I was quite resentful" of Jack's travels, she admitted. "When we first got engaged, Jack took off for Costa Rica to live on a resort on the Osa Peninsula to homeschool the son of an American expat who owned the resort. Jack was planning on spending nine months to a year there," she explained. "Being a new lawyer didn't allow me to take that kind of time off." Left at home, working her tail off at the law firm, Aileen felt "a bit deserted. Or if not that, at least I felt that I was the only responsible one. I was working, paying the bills, keeping the apartment, caring for his dog. For a number of reasons, Jack quit his gig in Costa Rica and decided to return to the States. Yet the experience certainly put a strain on our relationship and soured me a bit about his travels."

By 2005, Aileen realized that, while their arrangement might be OK for Jack, it wasn't OK for her. She was working all the time (or driving to and from work), and she felt like she was missing Gabby's childhood, years they could never get back. Further, they were concerned about the school system in El Granada, which was relatively poorly rated. They began to discuss a change in lifestyle, perhaps a move to a place that was more affordable and would allow Aileen to take some time off from practicing law. Jack agreed, but with one condition:

Their new home, wherever it was, needed good surfing nearby.

Three-Bed, Two Baths, and Six-Foot Swells

After months of research, Jack and Aileen decided on a house near Wilmington, North Carolina, a charming and affordable area just off the coast where there were sizable waves. (Sometimes too big: On a portion of the North Carolina coast that juts out into the Atlantic, Wilmington is often in the path of hurricanes.) They also agreed that Jack would return to teaching in some capacity while Aileen stayed home, at least for a while. In early 2006, they sold their house in El Granada, pocketed a decent profit, and moved to their new home on the East Coast.

Not surprisingly, it didn't take long for Jack to become ensconced in the local surfing community in Wrightsville Beach, a town dominated by "Surf Camp," perhaps the biggest and most famous surfing school in the country. Surf Camp combines summer-season surfing lessons for individuals and groups; a surfing day camp with an overnight component; and off-season "surf vacations" to places like Hawaii, Tortola, and Costa Rica.

Shortly after their arrival, Jack landed a job working at the camp, giving surfing lessons (after all, Aileen hadn't specified what *kind* of teaching he had to do). He soon became friendly with Rick Civelli, the owner, and before long he was offered a position as director of day camps and summer camps, which he accepted.

Today, Jack's obsession has finally become his profession. Even better, he gets paid to surf, without having to compete, and he gets to spend time teaching kids (and the occasional adult). "I'm able to travel abroad to teach surf lessons with this job as well, and I get paid!" Jack said. "And we are loving Wilmington!" Aileen works from home on part-time contract work for her California law firm, and the couple is now contemplating opening a day-care center too. Their lifestyle has been refocused on making sure they are both happy.

"What I would hope someone might learn is that life, not work, can be your priority," Jack said. "In this day and age of obesity, stress, and the almighty buck, there is a healthy alternative out there. There are paths that allow for more balanced lives. There are ways of organizing your life so that you can have time for your life." He continued, "My suggestion to people would be to make time for workouts, hobbies, friends, and family on a daily basis. Don't hope for it; ink it in to your daily schedule. When your boss asks you to stay longer at work, say 'NO!' They get ticked off, but they get over it, and they stop asking you after a while. If you get fired, then the job wasn't worth it," he said. "There can't be a higher priority than your own health. You have to maintain your health, physical or otherwise, to be worth anything to anybody else, anyway."

What about their family vacations? I asked Aileen. Was Jack allowed to bring his surfboard? "No!" she said adamantly. Yet, when describing a recent family cruise to the Caribbean, Jack mentioned the ship had made port in Barbados for a few hours. How was that? I asked.

"Great!" said Jack. "I borrowed a board, and the waves were pretty decent!"

10

A HARVARD PHYSICIAN GOES OFF THE GRID

ESCAPE ARTIST: JAMES LI
GREAT ESCAPE: FROM BOARDINGHOUSE
TO DOCTOR WITHOUT BORDERS

Imagine growing up thinking you're going to be an artist; losing your mother at the hands of a faith healer; dropping out of college to ride your bicycle across the country; deciding to go to medical school; and then ending up teaching at, of all places, Harvard. Then imagine giving up such a career in favor of creating a program to support doctors working in rural Africa. You sell your house, then you move to an uninhabited isle in service of a microeconomic experiment designed to determine if self-sufficiency for remote African villages is even possible.

Most of us expect our lives to move in less-than-obvious directions now and then. But some paths are *really* unlikely. And, as the story of James Li's career path shows, sometimes we need to take chances and follow seemingly risky courses to discover the thing we are really passionate about. Of course, some people are more ambitious than others in taking those risks: Considered selling the house and moving to an abandoned island lately? Like to learn how to dig your own well? James Li is nothing if not ambitious—some might say crazily so—but he's also a great example of a particular type of escape artist, one for whom getting away from the everyday is taken to its literal conclusion.

Brother, Can You Spare a Surgeon?

The plane banked abruptly and James Li, his eyes still closed, listened absently as the prop-driven engines changed their pitch from a steady whine to a lower, thrumming drone, the new sound a signal the flight from Kenya was coming to an end.

Opening his eyes after a somewhat fitful sleep, he glanced out the small window beside him. He saw nothing but blackness. His mind still moving slowly, it took him several seconds to register what he was seeing. Or not seeing. We must be over the ocean, he surmised. Though the flight from Nairobi to Freetown, Sierra Leone, had initially taken them across land— the vast, sparsely populated midsection of the African continent—the last section was over the Gulf of Guinea in the eastern Atlantic. The pilot must be approaching the capital port city from the west, the ocean side. That would explain the darkness below.

Looking more closely, his face pressed up against the scratched plastic of the plane's window, he was able to make out small pinpricks of light here and there, perhaps scattered fishing boats returning to Freetown. Though this would be his first visit, he knew a bit about Freetown's turbulent history. Now one of the largest cities in West Africa, the area that would become Freetown had been the center of the West African slave trade from 1650 until the late 1700s; many slaves began the Middle Passage at the busy port and landed at plantations in South Carolina and Georgia. In 1787, Sierra Leone was settled and established by slaves freed by the British; it would be nearly a century before neighboring Liberia, just to the south, would be founded by freed slaves from the United States. Rich in gold and diamonds, with a huge, strategically critical coastline on the North Atlantic, Sierra Leone had been a key piece of the British imperial puzzle carved into Africa during the eighteenth and nineteenth centuries. Freetown had been the capital of British West Africa for most of the 1800s, and Britain had maintained an important naval base there during World War II.

Virtually from the day of its founding, James recalled, the city had been in turmoil. Sacked by the French in 1794, burned by local tribes less than a decade later, Freetown was violently retaken by British forces during a bloody expansionist campaign that crossed the continent. The country was relatively calm until the 1960s, when a series of coups and countercoups began. In 1991, shortly before James's arrival, rebels (backed by Liberian strongman Charles Taylor) began attacking villages near the Liberian border, slowly encroaching on Freetown. By the mid-1990s Sierra Leone was, according to the United Nations Development Index, the poorest country in the world, a place where illnesses unknown in the industrialized world—typhus, malaria, dengue fever, tuberculosis—killed tens of thousands a year. And of course HIV and AIDS were rampant. And, James knew, infectious diseases were only part of the problem. The current civil war, though it had yet to reach the capital, had prompted the U.S. State Department to advise all aid groups to leave the country.

As the plane slowed and descended further, James briefly considered the likelihood that the driver assigned to take him to Masanga Leprosy Hospital—a trip to Sierra Leone's interior that would take at least six hours over rutted dirt roads—would show up. Then he let the thought pass. No sense in worrying about that now. He once again peered out into the night as he felt the customary bump and rattle of landing. He sensed something odd about the city, something that felt slightly off. Looking at his watch, which read midnight, he suddenly realized what it was. The blackness he had seen was not water, and the twinkling lonely lights were not fishermen. The plane had not been over the ocean. It had been sweeping over Freetown, across the city itself. Now he understood. Freetown, a city of more than a million people, had no electricity. There were no lights. The city was dark.

As he walked down the stairs from the plane and onto the tarmac, James saw a sea of faces surrounding the small airport entrance. The humidity hit him like a wall, as did the smells, a mixture of salt and dampness and the metallic odor of burning kerosene: Freetown residents carried it in milk tins and burned it for light. His official driver was nowhere to be found, but he was soon deluged with offers to drive him anywhere he wanted to go—including Masanga, which one helpful cab driver had noted was "only 20 minutes" from the airport. Other people offered—or demanded—to carry his bags, which were filled with medical equipment and supplies for Masanga. James decided to take a bus into the center of town.

As he sat, trying to keep his entire luggage within reach, a couple in their sixties, looking overheated and extremely confused, got on. They were clearly Americans, James noted, the husband in a golf hat and both man and wife looking very much like what they were, Americans trying to find their daughter, who was a mission doctor at an up-country hospital. Like James's driver, she too had not been there to greet them. The three Americans decided to travel together to the center of Freetown, hoping they would be able to connect with their contacts. After a long jolting ride, the bus stopped on a street lit only by the hundreds of milk tin handheld kerosene lanterns carried by Africans walking in the humid night air. The three tumbled out. Sure enough, the couple's daughter was there waiting. James introduced himself and explained where he was headed. Perhaps her hospital had a radio he could borrow to contact Masanga? The woman began to get excited.

"You're a doctor?" she asked hopefully.

"Well," James replied carefully, "Yes. That is, I'm a medical student. I mean, I just finished my fourth year." He hadn't even begun his residency, he told the woman. He was scheduled to perform his residency at Charity Hospital in New Orleans later that year. Then he added quickly, "But it's true I have an M.D."

"Do you know how to operate?" the woman inquired. Unsure where this line of inquiry was going, James admitted that he had performed a few basic surgical procedures in Kenya. Thank goodness, the woman replied. She was trained as a family physician and had no surgical skills, she said. Might James possibly be willing to come to her hospital instead of going to Masanga?

Oh, she added almost casually, and the hospital was desperately short staffed. Would James mind terribly taking over the hospital's operating theater?

An Escape from Communism

James Li was not among the kids who knew, growing up, that they wanted to become doctors. He was more interested in exploring the world, which he avidly did by foot, bicycle, train, and boat. Born in Seattle in 1965, James was a first-generation American. His mother was born during World War II in the Philippines, and she became a refugee after James's grandfather, a schoolteacher, was executed by the Japanese. His grandmother escaped to Hong Kong, where she started a sewing school, raised her three children, and then packed James's mother off to the United States for college when she turned 17. Born in Nanjing, China, James's father was also forced to escape when the communists invaded the country in 1949—James's grandfather worked for the Taiwanese Nationalist government and would have been executed had he stayed. "It's a wild background," James said. "Culturally, I'm an American, but I have enough roots to know what Chinese sounds like even though I can't speak it." As in many families with similar backgrounds, James's parents would speak Chinese at home when they didn't want their kids to know what they were discussing.

James's father was a civil engineer whose specialty was sewage treatment systems. His mother kept the house and raised her two children: James and his younger sister. When James was 14, his mother died of breast cancer. This tumultuous period was marked by two other memorable events: First, James took himself out of the private school that his mother had chosen and enrolled himself in the Seattle public school system, a paradoxical choice that began a "long and terrific education, in both book and street sense." Second, his father opened a student boardinghouse out of their home, giving James the opportunity to spend his teen years living with a diverse group of people.

Though Seattle today has a large Asian immigrant population, James recalled this period as the one when his family was the only "Li" in the phone book. "Today there are pages of them," he laughed. "Growing up, there were times when I was the only Asian American in school." That would change dramatically. During periods of political and economic uncertainty similar to the ones experienced by James's parents, many Asian families sought new lives in the United States. During his high school years, the city of Seattle accepted several thousand teenage refugees from the Vietnamese civil war. "Minorities became the majority in high school. I took a swimming class in the morning. The school bused in about 500 Vietnamese kids, mostly because they didn't know what else to do with them. Nobody spoke English. I made a lot of great friends that way."

James entered the University of Washington in 1983, and he had no idea what he was going to do. He took some Spanish and math courses, but he decided that it might be fun to learn how to sculpt or work with metal, or paint, so he declared a fine arts major, and he ended up in photography. Two years into college, he became disillusioned and dropped out. "I was working my way through, paying for it myself, and I realized that if I was just taking guitar and Spanish, it was a waste of money. I figured I'd get my head straight first and then I'd go back to it later if I wanted. So I outfitted a bicycle and spent a year traveling around the United States."

But You Can't Eat a Bike

James described this choice as "a great experience, something that probably made me much more reasonable and grounded than anything else I could have done." He left in the winter (a bit impractical for a bike trip, he admitted) and rode off down the West Coast. His father thought he was crazy, but James noted that "I don't think I was really in a position where I felt like I needed to explain myself, or negotiate what I wanted to do. I just figured 'this is something that sounds interesting; I don't know where it's going to lead.' And you know what? It taught me that with no money, and no plans, and not even an idea of where I'm going to sleep every night, life could still be really rich and fun. And it helped me realize that you are not stuck doing one thing."

In common with many of the other escape artists I met, as a young person James had a tendency to dismiss worries about money or else to place money in the context of the experiences it might afford rather than the things it could buy. And though as a doctor he would eventually go on to draw a larger salary—

albeit briefly—he never mentioned making lots of money as an especially important goal. "Looking back on it now, I realize there was a time in my life when I was living on $4,000 a year. It's nice to know that there was a period where I had an experience that actually showed me that there are other things that are more important than money, that it's not just about making a living."

His bike trip took him down the coast, through Texas (where he ran out of money), and then across the Deep South. Occasionally, he would cross paths with other cyclists, and they would travel together for a while. But more often, he was alone. One of the highlights of this period in his life, James said, was the tendency, particularly in the South, for strangers to stop by the side of the road, strike up a conversation, and invite him into their homes for a meal. I asked him if, as an Asian traveling by himself in the South, he recalled any notable experiences of racism. Interestingly, he cited his ethnicity as an attribute that conferred on him a sense of neutrality, something that allowed him to move between the black and white worlds of the South—worlds that were often very separate—with relative ease ("almost as if I was invisible, moving between two cultures"). In the occasional white household he would find himself being warned about "the blacks," while in some black households he was in turn warned about "the whites." Eventually, James landed in New Orleans, where he ended up crashing in an apartment filled with students and travelers who couldn't afford the $10 a day the local youth hostel charged. He stayed for several months, working odd jobs, before heading east and then up the East Coast; he would return to New Orleans for his residency some years later. He lived in New York for a while, and somehow he landed a job working for American Youth Hostels, with whom he got the chance to lead student groups through the United States and Europe for several years. "During the New York experience—and the reason I bring it up now—I met a lot of really great people who were all living what I think would be considered now as 'alternative' nontraditional lives," James said. "And they were very happy. And I've followed them and kept in touch with some of those people for the 20 years since, and they're doing as well as, or better than, most of the people that I know who are in a 'traditional' type of life."

Hearing about his obviously fond memories of this trip, it seemed to me that James might easily have given up school altogether and slipped into the wanderlust lifestyle early on, never to return to "real life." I wondered if perhaps there was a particular person or event that prompted James to return to college, later committing to medical school and then residency, and putting him well past 30 when he finally finished. Curiously, he credited his decision not to something that occurred during this period but rather to three young men who lived in his family's boardinghouse while he was growing up. Two were medical students, and one was a dental student. "They were just very gregarious, open people—they didn't seem like," he paused, "like *doctors*, like they should be doctors. It made me think that maybe medicine is not as bad as it seemed. In fact, it was a totally foreign field to me. I didn't know anyone who had gone into medicine." Looking back now he said, "It turned out to be rigorous in a good way. It's first a very intellectual, educational process. But you also get to meet and work and train with people who are really great. The interactions with people were very appealing. But the truth is, I had *no idea* that it would be so long a road."

There was, however, another event that played a role in the path his life would follow. When James was nine, his mother was diagnosed with advanced breast cancer. Both his parents were suspicious of Western medicine; some of this was cultural, James feels, probably because they had had experience with Asian "healers" and acupuncturists before they arrived in the United States. Eventually, she agreed to treatment at the University of Washington, after which she went into temporary remission. After getting sick again, she agreed to a randomized trial of an experimental drug, and she relapsed badly and blamed her doctors. Soon thereafter, she turned her back on Western medicine completely and, using the family's savings, went to Mexico to "detoxify" at a clinic run by a local healer whom James described as a "quack, an evil person at heart, an opportunist. When she died, it was from both her cancer as well as complications of the alternative therapy."

I asked James if, in retrospect, he felt these events helped lead him toward medicine as a profession. His answer was somewhat circumspect. "It definitely shook me up. But I don't think it really drove me to do the things I did, as much as I would like to say it could have. She was a very adventurous person herself, and maybe the lesson I learned is that it's hard to predict what's going to happen to you even five years down the road. If you're open enough to opportunities that come by, and you take them on wholeheartedly, sometimes great things that you never would have predicted happen to you. Things turn out well." I asked James if he felt the experience made him a better doctor. He replied that it probably did. "I don't know whether it's a truth for everyone or just for me, but seeing other people's suffering—and in large part this is what motivates me when I work in the developing world—if you can't actually acknowledge suffering, it's difficult to be compassionate and to actually practice medicine as a human being." He went on, "It's simple for doctors, with the education they have, to cook up a treatment scheme for anything. But connecting with another person as a human being is very difficult."

After traveling by bike for a year, James decided to move back to Seattle and finish school. After graduating, he enrolled in medical school at the University of Washington, and the trip down the long road began.

Working for Charity

Among the poor of New Orleans, Charity Hospital was known as "Big Charity," a place where medical care was always free, by design. Among its surgical residents, however, the hospital was known familiarly as a "knife and gun club." Before it was finally put out of business by Hurricane Katrina in 2005 after many years of criticism and mismanagement, Charity had been the oldest continually operating hospital in the United States. It was a bustling hospital serving as a literal lifeline for the indigent residents of New Orleans, one of the poorest cities in the nation. Founded by the state as a nonprofit hospital expressly to provide free medical care to the city's poor, Charity was typically the only option available to sick or injured residents who needed immediate and long-term care.

James chose the hospital for his residency because he knew and liked the city and he thought Charity would be a good place to learn the practicalities of emergency medicine. He recalled that he was the only person in his Seattle medical school class to head south for residency. At the time, Charity had the highest-volume emergency room in the country, and James spent about half his time there dealing with trauma (broken bones, stabbings, gunshot wounds). The rest of his time in the ER was spent dealing with a huge variety of medical problems—sometimes serious conditions such as heart attacks, other times less severe illnesses that more prosperous residents (those with health insurance, for example) might treat with a visit to the family doctor. He also rotated through other specialties, including orthopedics, neurosurgery, pediatrics, obstetrics, and surgery.

Emergency medicine is one of the few remaining specialties left in the United States in which residents still get a broad-based clinical education, with hands-on experience doing lots of different things (including some of the medical procedures I write about in my Worst-Case Scenario book series, which is how I came to know James in the first place). James noted that family medicine is a bit similar, though not quite as intense as working in the ER. Though such comprehensive medical training might be considered a throwback in the United States, medical care in the developing world remains a place for generalists, mostly because the illnesses and treatments vary so widely and the scarcity of trained doctors makes specialization a pointless luxury.

Getting into Harvard Is the Hardest Part

In early 1997, after finishing his training as chief resident, James began thinking about where he might like to live and work. At the time, he was dating a medical student who had been "matched" with a hospital in Boston for her residency. Deciding to stay together, he called around to see what hospitals in the area might have open positions for ER doctors, and he soon found a position with Mount Auburn, a community and teaching hospital affiliated with Harvard. "I had never thought I would go into medicine, and I certainly never thought I would be teaching!" James laughed. But he loved the job and the hospital, which offered wide-ranging experience in all sorts of medicine and constantly had a new crop of bright young Harvard medical students coming through. "I was teaching emergency medicine residents, and you have to understand that emergency medicine is a very small specialty—there are probably only a few hundred in the country—so everybody knew everybody else," James said. "It was really great." In addition to hands-on training, where the residents would actually diagnose and treat patients under his license, James began teaching emergency medicine in the classroom, as well as publishing articles in prestigious medical journals like *Lancet* and *Annals of Emergency Medicine*. "It was a surprise to me that I liked the teaching so much, but I felt it was very stimulating intellectually, and I got promoted [within the Harvard system]" he recalled. During this period, James began a new relationship with a blonde, blued-eyed woman named Kim, a lawyer. Ironically, Kim spoke fluent Mandarin (which James neither speaks nor understands), having spent the previous decade working in China and Hong Kong.

After working and teaching for eight years, James was easily able to picture a life in academic medicine, devoted to work, teaching, research, and publishing. It wasn't the future he wanted. "That sort of life is filled with constant unending work, with little room for other interests. Many people who do it are so focused, they become unidimensional," James said. But there was another reason he was hesitant to follow the path of an academic doctor. "The reward is prestige, something I never wanted for myself, a big name," he added. "That's just not who I was or wanted to be." Since 1992, he had been making regular, months-long trips to villages in Kenya, Tanzania, Ethiopia, and Malawi, practicing general medicine in remote regions. He felt he could do more good, and help more people, doing something similar with his life. "I went into medicine for the personal interactions," James said. An academic path seemed less than fulfilling. He wanted to use what he'd learned to provide direct assistance to people who needed it—not write research papers.

He began to think about creating some sort of organization that would place qualified, American-trained doctors in developing nations, in the small villages and hospitals where their services were most desperately needed. But the challenges facing such an effort were numerous. First, unlike existing medical and aid organizations, which are typically focused on emergency relief medicine, James knew that for long-term care in the developing world, it was critical that doctors have an "immersion" experience, to actually live and work in these places, getting a firsthand understanding of the care that was needed. Second, in order to attract U.S. doctors to, say, a six-month stay in a place like Ethiopia, he would need to offer tens of thousands of dollars to compensate them for the salary they'd be giving up by leaving their medical practices.

Third, even among those who wanted to go, finding qualified physicians would be difficult: The doctors would need not only experience with diagnosing and treating malaria, polio, tetanus, and other eradicable diseases but also the ability to deliver a breech baby or treat a farmer gored by a bull or perform brain surgery. It was a tall order. "In my experience working in Africa, I found the only people who had the ability to do all these things were mission doctors, and most of them were now in their seventies and eighties, and they were not being replaced by a younger generation," James said.

To make matters worse, in the new, post-9/11 landscape, much of the funding for such organizations had disappeared, or it had been redirected to security-related organizations. Nevertheless, James was undeterred. "[The] five-year plan was to write grants and [have enough money] to establish a permanent presence in a third-world hospital," he said. "I think I wrote 40 grant applications myself." He traveled back and forth to Africa, building relationships and liaisons with local hospitals, at the same time calling on like-minded colleagues to join a board of directors for his nonprofit, which he called "Remote Medicine." "I wanted it to have a structure so that at some point if I left, the organization would still be there," James recalled.

Eventually, he received grants of a few thousand dollars, enough to pay for the travel and living expenses of a few residents to live and work in the developing world. But there was still the problem of figuring out who would go. "It's funny because when I was at Harvard, I was involved in a NASA initiative to try to figure out how a mission to Mars would deal with medical care [for the astronauts]. Who would be qualified to perform all the various procedures that might be needed? What equipment would they use? We looked into using ultrasound instead of an X-ray machine to diagnose broken bones because an ultrasound machine weighed a lot less," he said, "and the thing was, these were the very same issues we were dealing with in trying to get good medical care to the developing world." Ultimately, James was astounded by the enormous interest in the available positions; there were hundreds of requests that typically came from doctors, medical residents, and students from all across the country.

But there was still one problem that did not have a solution. Yet. James felt that, ultimately, the poorest regions of the globe needed to become viably self-sufficient. Rather than rely on foreign aid distributed (or withheld) at the whim of the United States and other developed nations, such places needed local skills and resources to succeed (or at least get by) on their own. This meant not relying on the rest of the world for water or power or fuel or construction expertise or well drilling. And if one of his goals was to help poor regions figure out how to do all of this, then he'd need to learn quite a bit himself about living "off the grid."

So in 2002, he and Kim decided on their escape. They packed up their things, took leaves from their jobs, and moved north and east, to an uninhabited island off the coast of Maine.

Deserted, but No Desert

The islands scattered in the North Atlantic off the Maine coast were among the first areas of the country to be settled, typically by fishermen who sailed from Scandinavia in the 1600s. James and Kim had heard about a rocky islet of just 150 acres that had appeared on the earliest, British-made charts of the coastal area between Brunswick and Rockland. Up until 1940, the island had a formal village and was populated year-round, mostly by commercial lobstermen and their families. But by 1955, the local elementary school had shuttered and moved to the mainland, mail service was discontinued, and homeowners got on their boats and left. Today, nature has taken over most of what humans created, and roads are gone, hidden under wild grasses and brush. The harsh winters have left little but foundations of the houses that once peppered the island. A few homes remain, but they are used only seasonally, by the families who are the descendants of the original lobstermen—and who are lobstermen themselves.

"We made a conscious decision to make a philosophical change in how we were living," James recalled. "And it was also a microeconomic experiment, to see if we could live using the systems crucial to the developing world: active and passive solar energy systems, composting toilets, well water, satellite communications systems, and small-plot farming." In 2002, using savings and the money obtained from selling their home, they purchased a small hundred-year-old house on the island. This one had no electricity, running water, septic system, or even insulation. "The top floor was just totally open," James said and laughed. "The snow would just blow right in!" Their idea was to live through a winter on the island despite the elements, without the usual utility services, and with the possibility of total isolation during periods when the island became inaccessible due to the surrounding sea ice. "We wanted to see if it was livable, to see if we could make a home from systems that we eventually could put to work in the developing world."

Immediately, they invested in equipment they would need. They put up a 10-panel solar array and connected it to a 2,000-pound rack of batteries, which were stored in a shed. To meet the electrical household requirements, James wired the house to run off inverters connected to the batteries. He hooked up a marine storage tank with a hand pump, and the two of them filled it every three days from a hand-dug well. Eventually, he wired a pump from a deeper well and plumbed water to a faucet, doing all the plumbing himself. With help from a local carpenter, he began learning construction techniques and began making improvements to the house itself, adding insulation and closing off the openings in the upper floor. Refrigeration and stove cooking came from propane and a low-wattage chest freezer they installed in the stone cellar. Light came from propane lanterns and rechargeable LED headlamps. Heat was supplied from a wood-burning stove but one that was sufficient only to heat a single room. They used the stove to heat water for bathing and cooking, and eventually they found a larger replacement that a neighbor helped haul from the mainland by lobster boat. James bought and learned how to pilot and repair a small diesel lobster boat, the only way to get to and from the island. He learned to operate a tractor. "We looked into putting in a wind-powered generator, but the island is in a protected area without much wind."

What if there was a medical emergency and they needed help, I wondered. James, of course, had set up a small clinic during the warmer months for the summer residents. As for the winters, when the island could be inaccessible from December through February (even by helicopter, because there was no sufficient landing site), he was confident that he could handle all but the most severe injury himself—though in my mind I pictured him lying bleeding on a table holding a mirror to his leg, directing Kim, through clenched teeth, on emergency cauterization.

The summer locals, of course, thought they were crazy for staying on the island year-round. But that didn't mean they weren't willing to help out. "I remember finding creosote stains on the outside of the chimney one day. I was afraid the flue was cracked and we were going to have a chimney fire and burn the place down," James said. "So I asked around, and I found the man who had actually built the chimney. He was older and in a wheelchair. Kim went and visited him and got instructions on how to fix it." Many of the islanders, like James, had become self-sufficient partly out of choice, but mostly out of necessity, and there were people who knew how to fix almost anything. But come September, the locals went home to the mainland, leaving James and Kim alone with the nonhuman island inhabitants: birds, squirrels, and a lone 15-year-old fox. And the mosquitoes, though they turned out to be a blessing in disguise.

Many of the regions James was seeking to help were plagued by epidemics of malaria, a disease spread by mosquito bites. As a part of his living experiment, he had the opportunity to fine-tune his mosquito control strategies. "I've tried almost everything—killing the larvae, spraying, permethrin derivatives, repellants, netting, even commercial mosquito traps." His is powered by propane and "actually works pretty well!" he said, laughing.

That first winter was cold, with temperatures as low as –25°F, before the windchill. The island was iced in from December to February, and of course there were only a few hours of hazy daylight per day, not direct sun. To their amazement, the solar and battery arrays did their jobs well, collecting and storing enough energy to run the household—which included satellite Internet service, a wireless network, a cell phone, a stereo, and a television. Internet service enabled Kim to run a virtual law office from their home, from which she negotiated business contracts for international companies. Their systems even allowed her to videoconference for "face-to-face" meetings. For James, it enabled him to run Remote Medicine, stay in touch with colleagues, and keep up with current events.

Lobster? Again?

After surviving their first two winters, the couple decided to live on their island year-round. In 2005, James resigned his faculty appointment at Harvard and took a job in the emergency room at Miles Memorial Hospital in Damariscotta, a small but well-equipped community hospital in central Maine. On his workdays, he walks to the beach, pulls in a dingy attached to a line, and then rows out to the lobster boat. From there, it's a 40-minute "commute" to the coast to a parked truck. Then it's a 45-minute drive to the hospital. Some nights, after his shift ends, James sleeps at the hospital; lately he's arranged to stay at friends' houses when they are away for the season. He spends his off days gardening ("not going so well," he said), designing a hot water system; and improving the house. As of this writing, he has passive solar water-heating panels and most but not all of the parts to pump hot water to the house. Winters are long and cold, though the 2005–2006 winter was mild enough that their island was not iced in, making travel to the mainland possible. James has also learned how to trap lobster and crab—admittedly not a skill that's readily applicable in Africa but fun nonetheless—and summers he and Kim lay in a good supply. For now, they have no children, and they both realize that adding kids to the mix would make their simple life infinitely more complex. Though their initial plan was to live on the island temporarily, until their "experiment" in self-sufficiency was complete, James said they now plan to live there permanently. I asked if perhaps their choice was a lonely one. James said, surprisingly, that it wasn't. "You know, it's just so beautiful here, so unspoiled, I wake up in the morning and sometimes I'm overwhelmed by the serenity."

The one thing that's missing is the travel abroad. The off-grid experiment and transition from urban to rural life have so fully occupied them that James has not been back to Africa for two years. "Ultimately, our goal is to work and live here for six months, saving enough to live in Africa for the rest of the year or longer," he said. "The next time I go, I'll take Kim, and we'll move as if we're not coming back." He hopes the skills he is learning on his island will in time be usable both by Remote Medicine's own doctors and by the rural patients they serve. Having such basic necessities as self-sufficiently produced power, water, agriculture, sewage treatment, and mosquito control can, James believes, go a long way toward eventually making medical care in the developing world more preventive and less crisis oriented.

In the meantime, James said, Remote Medicine is "mature enough to give other doctors the opportunity to experience [in Africa] what I've experienced. Hopefully, we can encourage others to make the same philosophical changes we have in our lives, with the same goal of an eventual life serving communities in the third world."

CONCLUSION

How to Make
Your Escape

Traditional "business" books typically conclude with a gift to the reader: a nice little box of expert wisdom, wrapped in the guise of universal truths, applicable to any and all business situations. Admittedly, this formula is popular because it's appealing. People like to hear that the world of work is the same everywhere and that success is just a few easy-to-digest concepts, a few "tipping points" away. If you only follow these simple rules, the authors seem to say, you'll realize that all jobs have the same fundamental characteristics.

Who Moved My Cheesy Business Book?

If you've gotten this far, you know that this is anything but a typical business book. Since I've written a nontraditional book about unusual careers, a book about different people involved in offbeat jobs—call it an "antibusiness" business book—it seems fitting somehow that I'm resistant to offering such universal truths about escape artists. There won't be any "Seven Rules of Highly Effective Clowns" or "The 10-Day Navy SEAL." Each escape artist is unique, each situation different, and that's actually part of the point. This book is all about finding what works for *you* and *your* situation, not about what has to work for everyone everywhere. It's a book about individuals, for individuals.

A few years ago, when I began thinking about the concept that would eventually become *The Escape Artists*, I worried briefly about what conclusions I might realistically pull together after writing it. After all, 10 people are hardly a representative sampling of the general population, statistically or otherwise. And, of course, I'm not a sociologist, statistician, or practiced cultural observer seeking to create some new theory explaining everything about everyone for all time. (Actually, I'm really just a guy who likes to interview people with cool jobs.) I also wasn't necessarily looking to provide the definitive guide to people who put their passions first all the time, to the detriment of the rest of their lives; our passions can certainly get the better of us if we don't keep them in check (at least sometimes!).

Those are a few of the things I *didn't* want to do. What I *did* want to accomplish was at once simpler and a bit more difficult: I wanted to find and tell the stories of interesting people who, like me, have found creative ways to make a living "outside the cubicle." Because, let's face it, we're not all cut from the same career cloth. For some (perhaps many) of us, working at an office job isn't something we aspire to. We'll do it, if and when we have to, but we can't picture ourselves doing it our entire lives. The rise of the Internet and the ability to communicate from virtually anywhere at any time has shaped a generation of young people who don't necessarily see a need—or have a desire—to be tied to a desk. And even many older workers, those who came to the Internet later in life, have similarly discovered the joys of freedom of location, whether that means telecommuting from a home office or running a business from a boat. The freedom to leave the office is also the freedom to spend time with family and friends or to pursue other interests. There is now a refreshingly widespread mindset that "work" can be at once broader, more fulfilling, and more interesting. It can be whatever, wherever, and whenever we want it to be.

The "French" Way

Someone once told me that when you ask an American about herself, she'll talk about what she does. But when you ask a French person the same question, he'll talk about *who he is*; that is, he'll talk about his personal interests, hobbies, and family. This contrast reflects differing cultural attitudes toward work and probably isn't precisely true (or true all the time, or anymore). Regardless, it still sounds pretty good. Why can't we let who we are be defined by our interests, by what we really care about? That's not to imply there aren't millions of people out there who are jazzed to get up every day and, say, gaze at a spreadsheet or pore through stacks of legal documents or peer into a microscope. There are people like that, and that's fine.

But the escape artists profiled in this book tend to have more active interests outside the mainstream, workaday world, and that's what separates them from people who perform jobs they may like but are not passionate about.

But the question remains. Are there common denominators among an extreme skier, a third-world physician, a clown, a pitcher, a Trekkie? Among a surfer, a rafter, a DEA agent, a Navy SEAL, a comedian? Trying to pinpoint specific characteristics they all share is difficult. We could look to their upbringings, but they too were all quite different: Some had supportive parents, some had parents with very specific expectations (typically unmet), and some had parents who stayed married, others who divorced. Some had very difficult childhoods; some didn't. What about schooling? Again, the threads don't always connect: Some went to public school, some private; some did well, some didn't do especially well; some finished college, some didn't (though they did all finish high school). They are not all men or all women or all white or all nonwhite. And they grew up all over the country (or in other countries), under varied financial conditions.

So, *do* they connect? Do they share common characteristics? I think they do, at least to some extent. They are all adamant that they could never envision themselves happy in an "office" or "regular" job. Most of them are less than thrilled with the idea of working for and answering to someone else—though of course on some level we're all answerable to the one who pays us. They like to do things they feel are worthwhile, things that make people happy—whether that means making *Star Trek* phasers for fans, giving free medical care to the indigent, teaching surfing, or catching drug dealers. The escape artists in this book tend to be creative people and problem solvers, and they also tend to be independent thinkers—people who would rather figure things out on their own than be told how things are (and when they are told, they tend to be skeptical). Most have found ways to balance time spent on their passions with time for family, which is not an easy task for anyone.

It's important to keep in mind that escape artists don't necessarily start out that way. For example, when I graduated from college in 1993, I thought I'd be happy with an office job, so I settled into entry-level publishing, first in New York, then later in Los Angeles. It took a few years for me to realize that going to and from a cubicle—and sitting in one for eight hours a day—began to make me feel dead inside. I knew I wanted to write, but I didn't realize initially that I wanted to do it in my own way, on my own time, and without a boss and fluorescent lighting hanging over me. Similarly, some of the people featured in this book had "normal" careers before coming to the realization that they weren't precisely *normal*—or at least that what they wanted to do didn't fit within the bonds of convention. Sometimes people have to try things they hate to discover what they really love and feel passionate about. And sometimes simply doing what we love to do (skiing, surfing, white-water rafting) can lead to a fulfilling career (filmmaking, teaching surfing, travel writing) that we might not have anticipated and that might even financially support our "escape." And isn't it so cool when that happens?

What Price, Escape?

No endpaper to this book would be complete without at least a brief discussion of money: specifically, following your passion and discovering that you don't have any. Gaining the freedom to do what we want when we want has a price, and that price can sometimes (though not always) be measured in dollars. Mark Divine left a comfortable job on Wall Street for the Navy. Karen DeSanto left a government job and her own business behind to join the circus. Chuck Bechtel is earning poverty wages pitching a baseball. I have to pay my own health insurance—and it's a major drag. But being happy in what you do helps to make up for added difficulty in other parts of life, and escape artists generally are willing to make this sacrifice in exchange for personal and professional fulfillment. Just ask James Li.

And, of course, for escape artists with families, there's always the relative weighting of personal fulfillment versus what a spouse and children are willing to put up with and make time and sacrifices for. Steve Smith has finally found a career he loves, but his wife is finding the unpredictable hours a difficult adjustment. Rich Coyle divorced his first wife and became estranged from his children because of his passion for *Star Trek*. Chuck Bechtel may finally have to leave a baseball career behind so he can support his family. Ultimately, each person's situation is unique, and we all have lines and boundaries forcing us to make hard choices that, in a perfect world, we wouldn't have to make. But I think most of the subjects in this book would argue that a big part of their inner peace stems from having a supportive family, one that allows them to pursue professional and personal growth on their own terms. Even if that means sacrifice.

I tend to avoid books with explicit messages, morals, life-changing stratagems, and the like. (If you want those, may I suggest Dr. Phil?) I don't profess to have all the answers—or even most of them—to the question of what makes people pursue their passions and find success in doing so. But if you picked up this book, my guess is you're looking less for easy answers and more for ideas and examples—real people with interesting stories to get you thinking about what life can be like on an alternative track, one that goes beyond the cubicle walls. You may be just starting a career or thinking of changing an existing one or even preparing to retire and looking for a change in future course. (I recently met a woman whose husband retired from finance and now drives an ambulance!) Whatever you're doing and in whatever stage of life you're doing it, my hope is that after you put this book down, you'll have at least some new perspective on what can happen when you pursue your passion. It's a road that, at least anecdotally, more and more people are willing to travel, even though it's generally not an easy journey—and the end is typically uncertain. But life is full of risks, and the best rewards often come to those willing to take them.

Twenty years ago, when I was still in high school, someone once gave me some great advice (and I distinctly recall it wasn't my parents): "Do what you love; then find a way to make a living doing it." That's still pretty much on the mark, I believe, although I also remember a quip from that great ski filmmaker and part-time sage, Warren Miller: "Don't take life too seriously. You'll never come out of it alive." Putting both these bits of wisdom together, we end up with something like, "Do what you love, have fun doing it, and worry about the money later."

And that, I think, is exactly right.

NOTES

Chapter 2

33 *The principles of love*   See the Web page www.seido.com/
01_about_seido/kaicho.htm for more information about
this fascinating form of martial arts. Nakamura is still
teaching Seido karate throughout the United States and
the world, and he has 20,000 students.

36 *I started to read about the SEALs*   Mark recently
found out that Jeff Schaeffer was actually in Explosives
Ordnance Disposal and not in the SEALs.

38 *At the end of the summer*   Interestingly, Woodruff and
his wife were the founders of the Ultraman Triathlon, in
Hawaii.

40 *Much of the training*   Some of the detail in the section
comes from Mark's Web site, NavySEALS.com, and the
SOCOM Handbook.

Chapter 4

101 *It's too early to tell*   www.skateboard.about.com/od/
events/a/Olympics.htm.

Chapter 5

111 *Circus performers are not unionized*   Information on Clown College comes from Karen herself, her husband Greg (who is also a clown and who attended Clown College), and an article in the *Shawnee News-Star*, "Ringling Brothers: It's Time for a Tougher Clown Course," *Shawnee News-Star*, January 29, 1998.

112 *Ringling Bros. was the only game in town*   "In Daring Leap, Ringling Loses Its Three Rings," *The New York Times*, December 31, 2005, p. A-1. At the end of 2005, Kenneth Feld announced that one of the two Ringling Bros. shows would move to a no-ring format and add a storyline to its performances. Though he indicated the change was spurred not by competition from Cirque du Soleil but because Americans were already too distracted and looking for an emotional connection to their entertainment, many observers speculated that the circus was fearful of losing ticket sales to Cirque. At the time of this writing, it was too early to tell if the new format would succeed and become permanent for both Ringling tours.

122 *And, of course, circus*   "In Daring Leap, Ringling Loses Its Three Rings."

Chapter 7

148 *The Cagayan also wends its way*   Some of the details on this page come from the Philippines Tourism Board, at www.tourism.gov.ph, as well as American Whitewater, at www.americanwhitewater.org. The description of the

food comes from an article in *Outside* magazine, written by Steven Rinella: http://outside.away.com/outside/ destinations/2002travelguide/2002travel_guide_ philippines_rafting_1.adp.

150 *Loosely translated* www.world66.com/asia/south eastasia/philippines/kalinga.

159 *One morning, a few days into their trip* This story is adapted from a piece Bridget wrote for the Patagonia clothing company, published in their fall 2002 catalog, p. 59. Used with permission of the author.

Chapter 8

177 *Margaret Cho was directed* The detail about *All American Girl* comes from *The Encyclopedia of Gay, Lesbian, Bisexual, Transgender, and Queer Culture* (www.glbtq.com/arts/chom,2.html) and the *Internet Movie Database* (imdb.com).

ACKNOWLEDGMENTS

Obviously, thanks and good karma go out to all the subjects profiled in the book, without whom, well, there would be no book. I am grateful for your time and patience, for your good humor, for your interesting lives, and for your willingness to talk about sometimes difficult and personal events. Keep on escaping! A special thank you to Colin McAndrew of the Camden Riversharks for all the help in not only putting me in touch with Chuck and others but also in answering all my game-day questions with aplomb. Go Sharks!

Additionally, thanks to everyone at McGraw-Hill and especially Melissa Bonventre and Janice Race for helping to transform an idea into a manuscript and a manuscript into an actual book, with all the hours and days of work and discussion and debate that that entails. As always, thanks to my wife, Christine, and my agent, David Hale Smith, for the usual support and encouragement.

INDEX

ABOUT THE AUTHOR

Josh Piven is the author of 15 nonfiction books, including The Worst-Case Scenario Survival Handbook series and *As Luck Would Have It*. He made his escape from the cubicle in 1995 and now works from his couch—occasionally in his pajamas. He and his family live in Philadelphia.